Facing the Darkness and
Finding the Light

Facing the Darkness and
Finding the Light

Reflections for troubled times from
the book of Revelation

DAVID WINTER

Text copyright © David Winter 2011
The author asserts the moral right
to be identified as the author of this work

Published by
The Bible Reading Fellowship
15 The Chambers, Vineyard
Abingdon OX14 3FE
United Kingdom
Tel: +44 (0)1865 319700
Email: enquiries@brf.org.uk
Website: www.brf.org.uk
BRF is a Registered Charity

ISBN 978 1 84101 835 5
First published 2011
10 9 8 7 6 5 4 3 2 1 0
All rights reserved

Acknowledgments
Unless otherwise stated, scripture quotations are taken from the New Revised Standard
Version of the Bible, Anglicised Edition, copyright © 1989, 1995 by the Division of Christian
Education of the National Council of the Churches of Christ in the United States of America,
and are used by permission. All rights reserved.

Scripture quotations taken from the Revised Standard Version of the Bible, copyright © 1946,
1952, 1971 by the Division of Christian Education of the National Council of the Churches of
Christ in the United States of America, are used by permission. All rights reserved.

Scripture quotations taken from the Holy Bible, New International Version, copyright © 1973,
1978, 1984, 1995 by International Bible Society. Used by permission of Hodder & Stoughton
Publishers, a member of the Hachette Livre UK Group. All rights reserved. 'NIV' is a registered
trademark of International Bible Society. UK trademark number 1448790.

Extracts from the Authorised Version of the Bible (The King James Bible), the rights in which
are vested in the Crown, are reproduced by permission of the Crown's Patentee, Cambridge
University Press.

'Parousia' from *Swimming in the Flood*, copyright c 1995 John Burnside, published by Jonathan
Cape.

A catalogue record for this book is available from the British Library

Printed in Singapore by Craft Print International Ltd

Contents

*

Introduction

This book probably needs a bit of explanation. It isn't a commentary on Revelation, though it does take the reader through that strange and mesmerising book. It isn't a book of Bible readings, although passages from the Bible are set out from time to time to act as signposts and background to the argument. And it isn't, in one sense, a devotional book, although I hope that one consequence of reading it would be that faith is strengthened and trust in the God of history renewed.

What it is, in fact, is an extended treatment of a continuing puzzle for all of us, believers and non-believers alike. Where does evil come from? Why is it present in the world and within our own lives? Why do the innocent suffer and, too often, the crudely powerful prevail? If God exists and he is good (and the default position of this book is that he does and is), how can it be that the world he created seems to be constantly marred by conflict, war and natural disaster?

They are huge questions and human beings have asked them from the early days of the history of our race. It would be presumptuous to suggest that this short book is going to answer them to everybody's satisfaction, and I do not claim that it will. But there do seem to be in the book of Revelation (or 'Apocalypse', its Greek name) valid and helpful clues towards answers that the visionary nature of that book, and our difficulty in decoding it, may tend to obscure.

More than any other book in the Christian scriptures, those very questions are at its heart. Revelation is not for the squeamish, simply because the visions themselves, and the recording of them by John the seer, face the awfulness of much of human life head on. If we are to discover how to find some place of serenity and faith in the world as it is, we won't achieve it by shutting our eyes to reality. No one could accuse Revelation of doing that.

So this journey through its mysterious and often horrific visions will not be an easy one, but neither will it be futile. Somewhere in this maelstrom of passion, in there among the blood and horses and beasts from the pit, the light of divine purpose, hope and love shines. We shall face the darkness over these pages, but we shall also find the light.

A suggestion

It's possible, and you may prefer, to read this book without constant recourse to the text of Revelation, as relevant passages from it are given at the start of each chapter. However, if you are not already familiar with Revelation, you might find it helpful to read the whole of its 22 chapters before embarking on this book. Hold tight, though. It's a scary experience at times!

The human dilemma

'Do not worry about tomorrow, for tomorrow will bring worries of its own. Today's trouble is enough for today.'
MATTHEW 6:34

'Don't worry' has always seemed to me a very dubious piece of advice—indeed, often counterproductive. If the doctor at the hospital, who has in her hands the results of your recent tests, begins the conversation with the words, 'Now I don't want to worry you', you have a sneaking suspicion that the next word will be 'but': '... but we'd like to run some more tests' or '... but I'd like you to see my colleague in oncology.' Being told not to worry tends to imply that there is something to worry about, and that's all most of us need to embark on an orgy of anxiety.

If I regard 'don't worry' as pointless or even unhelpful advice, how do I reconcile that with the fact that Jesus himself constantly urged his followers not to be anxious? In one of the best-loved passages in the Sermon on the Mount, he lists all the things they shouldn't worry about—food, clothes, appearance, health or what might happen 'tomorrow' (Matthew 6:25–34). However, if there is no money in the purse, no food in the cupboard, no clothes in the wardrobe and I or someone I love has just been told we are seriously ill, surely I've got every reason to worry? As for 'tomorrow', isn't it natural to be a bit anxious about what might lie unanticipated just around the corner of life?

The answer of Jesus to all of these everyday, common-or-garden anxieties is to put them in perspective—to 'strive first for the kingdom of God and his righteousness' (v. 33), and then 'all these things' (food, clothes, health and so on) 'will be given to you'. As Jesus was clearly not offering a blanket guarantee of endless supplies of food and clothes or lifelong perfect health, the implication of his words must be that, set against the promise of the kingdom, such things assume a less dominant role in our lives. As the apostle Paul put it some years later:

I have learned to be content with whatever I have. I know what it is to have little, and I know what it is to have plenty. In any and all circumstances I have learned the secret of being well-fed and of going hungry, of having plenty and of being in need. I can do all things through him who strengthens me. (Philippians 4:11–13)

The teaching of Jesus and the practice of the apostle provide a key to unravelling the apparently mysterious message of the visions of Revelation. They too are about human suffering, need, fear and anxiety—much of it going far beyond worries about food, clothes or even health. The visions crash in with their images of a world of pain and distress, of war and tumult and plague and death. In one sense, especially to those of us who, through affluence or geographical location, are spared many of the worst of these horrors, both natural and of human creation, they may seem exaggerated—fictional terrors to be treated as remote from everyday experience.

From time to time, though, fictional terrors become everyday experience, as they did in Haiti in January 2010, and, a few weeks later, on the beautiful holiday island of Madeira. Earthquake and flood are not of human invention, and those who suffered were not guilty of sin to any greater extent than the residents of, say, Tunbridge Wells or Geneva. Unless our faith can accommodate the reality of human suffering and relate it to our understanding of a God of mercy, truth and love, we are living an escapist fantasy rather than the life of faith.

Three thousand years ago, the psalmist spoke of fearing 'the terror of the night, or the arrow that flies by day, or the pestilence that stalks in the darkness, or the destruction that wastes at noonday' (Psalm 91:5–6). The fears and anxieties of our day, however, are of a different kind. It's easy to see why people of biblical times were anxious in a world where hunger, poverty, violence and premature death were part of everyday experience. Of course, there is still violence in the world, as well as the occasional but devastating impact of natural disaster—tsunami, earthquake and flood—but today an increasingly large part of the world's population enjoys a degree of security and prosperity, health care and domestic comfort known only to the richest people of previous ages.

Nevertheless, we are a deeply troubled and anxious generation, troubled about aspects of daily life but even more about what might be coming to us. The problem, in the language of the Sermon on the Mount, is not today but 'tomorrow'. We feel not so much deprived, frightened or terrorised as helpless, like passengers on an aircraft that has no pilot or whose computers have failed.

During Advent 2009, the History Channel on British television offered as its autumn series 'The Seven Days of the Apocalypse'. This programme sought to answer the question of whether the book of Revelation in the Bible and similar writings about the end of the world were, in their words, 'prophetically true or a load of old mumbo-jumbo'. In fact, I suspect that the series left half its viewers confused and the other half apprehensive, introduced to a whole set of fears and anxieties that they had hitherto been spared. *2012*—a major film on the theme of the apocalypse, the final climactic disaster of the planet and its inhabitants—was released at about the same time. It is one of nine apocalyptic films currently available on DVD or in the cinema. The end of the world or, at any rate, of life as we know it, is presented to us as the scenario of the ultimate horror film, and in many ways it is. Television and cinema, as well as some popular writers of science fiction, have made the word 'apocalyptic' into a synonym for utter and unavoidable disaster.

Faced with all of this, what does the 'ordinary' person do? For many, the answer is to acquire a lottery ticket and hope that it's possible to buy one's way out of disaster. For others, perhaps most people, the simplest response is to go on living exactly as we have always done and try to ignore all the prophets of doom around us. Perhaps, if we do, it will all just go away. Put unkindly, this is the classic 'head in the sand' response. Some go to the doctor and collect antidepressants. Others, often our finest and our best, dedicate themselves to campaigning about this and that issue of the moment, joining pressure groups, petitioning their Members of Parliament and staging protests.

For many people, a catastrophe like the Haiti earthquake or the relentless warnings of possible future disasters raise serious questions about the existence of a loving God. How can Christians, they ask, continue to believe in a divine being who allows such appalling things to happen to his innocent creatures? On the streets of Port au Prince on the Sunday after the earthquake, however, many open-air masses were being celebrated, with thousands of people joining in the songs of worship: 'Holy, holy, holy, Lord God of hosts! Heaven and earth are full of your glory. Hosanna in the highest!' '*Full of your glory*'? As the stench of death filled the air, it mingled with the incense and the songs of the faithful. How can we account for this stark paradox?

It seems that in all of our fears, anxieties and sorrows—real or perceived—people are looking for a message of hope from somewhere. We are desperate for someone, anyone, to tell us that the situation is not completely out of control, that there is a way ahead, that there are genuine, solid grounds for hope. It also seems that we are searching for an answer, an explanation. How can it be that, in a world created by a good God, there is so much suffering, so much despair?

My suggestion in this book will be that those grounds for hope and that most elusive of all 'answers' can perhaps be found in the very book of the Bible, Revelation (Apocalypse), that provides the adjective we use to describe human catastrophes and disaster: 'apocalyptic'. Revelation is often represented as foretelling the end of the world. In fact, though, it is about the beginning of a new world, what Jesus called 'the kingdom of God'.

Revelation is the last book of the Bible—its 'last word', as it were, to the world. Today, it is largely known (if it is known at all) for its gruesome visions of plague, war and pestilence, brought by the deadly 'four horsemen of the Apocalypse' and the beast from the bottomless pit, culminating in the final battle of Armageddon. Yet for the man, John, who first described these visions, and for the people who read or heard them in those far-off days, hidden within the images of terror and violence was a glorious affirmation of the final triumph of good over evil. In the language of vision, it offered both an explanation of the presence of suffering and evil in God's creation and a message of profound hope to a troubled people. Believe it or not, Revelation is a book of timeless optimism.

That generation, or, rather, the particular group of people to whom the book was addressed, were also fearful. They lived in the first century of the Christian era. For the infant Church, storm clouds were brewing. Already, the might of imperial Rome had been pitted against Christians during the reign of Nero, probably more than 20 years before the book was written. Thousands had been martyred—fed to lions, crucified, slain in the arena by armed gladiators. Jesus had spoken of a new life, a kingdom of justice, peace and love. What had happened to that vision? Were his followers now abandoned to the whim of a mighty secular power? They knew that what had already happened could well happen again, and even more ferociously. They seemed so few, so powerless, so helpless in the face of the tide of events.

It was to such people, in a fast-changing world, that this strange and magnificent message of hope was delivered. They were as familiar as we are with the disasters, natural and man-made, that afflict the human race. After all, it's quite possible that the eruption of Vesuvius and the catastrophic fate of Pompeii and Herculaneum occurred at about the time that these words were written.

Revelation was couched in coded and, at times, obscure language and images, although people then were more familiar with this style of writing than are later generations. Hidden within its words, pictures and visions, however, the eye of faith could discern hope and triumph. They had not been forgotten by God.

We have not been forgotten, either. In a strange way, our present generation, increasingly familiar with literary and cinematic images of allegory, fantasy and horror, may be able to read Revelation with fresh insight. If we do, then we shall find in this mysterious and largely unread book the final message of the scriptures. The last word of God is not about judgment or inexplicable suffering and destruction, but about justice, meaning and purpose. It is a message of hope for the present, and for the future a vision of the inevitable victory of good over evil.

The defining vision: the risen Christ

Revelation 1

John, on the isle of Patmos, has a vision of the risen Jesus and is told, 'Write what you have seen, what is, and what is to take place after this' (v. 19).

'Do not be afraid; I am the first and the last, and the living one. I was dead, and see, I am alive for ever and ever.'
REVELATION 1:17–18

The book of Revelation is the written record of a series of visions given to a man called John who was exiled on the island of Patmos, in the Mediterranean. It was a Sunday—the 'Lord's day'—and he tells us that he was 'in the spirit' (v. 10), presumably a trance-like state of spiritual awareness. A loud voice told him to write in a book what he saw and to send it to seven churches in the Roman province of Asia (modern Turkey, more or less). From this vivid experience came the last book of the Christian scriptures.

John's first vision was of the risen Christ—a glorified,

terrifying spectacle; a figure human yet heavenly, holding in his right hand seven stars. Emanating from his mouth was a 'sharp, two-edged sword' (v. 16), a familiar biblical metaphor for the word of God (see, for example, Ephesians 6:17). We can compare this vision with those in Daniel 7:9–10 and 13–14. 'Son of Man' (*ben adam*, in Hebrew) is the title Jesus took to himself (see, for instance, Matthew 8:20; Mark 2:28; Luke 5:24). It can mean simply 'human being' but, as Jesus used it, the title seems to stand for rather more—perhaps himself as the 'representative' human person, what Luther called the 'Proper Man'.

Overawed, John fell to the feet of the figure, 'as though dead' (v. 17), but the man—beyond doubt, Jesus—raised him to his feet with one hand, saying, 'Do not be afraid; I am the first and the last, the living one. I was dead, and see, I am alive; and I have the keys of Death and of Hades'. Hades is not 'hell', a place of punishment, but simply the grave, the abode of the dead, where in later Jewish thought the departed spirits awaited the resurrection on the last day. To have the keys of Death is to claim authority over the event that brings life to an end. To have the keys of Hades is to claim the right to release those who have been its victims.

Those words set the tone of the whole book that is to follow: indeed, it can be truly understood only if seen from the perspective of that astonishing claim. As we read visions of conflict, horror, rampant evil and holy martyrdom, we need to do so with this glorious image of the risen Jesus before our eyes. It is Christ, not the enemies of God, who has the keys of death and the grave. Those who first heard the message of the book, and we who read it now, would need to know right from the start that this was not a vision of horror and defeat. They (and we) were not to be afraid, because the risen Jesus has conquered our last two enemies, sin and death.

Although John's visions start with the situation of the Church at that time and end with the final vision of the kingdom of heaven in all its glory, it's not quite true to say that the book traces a tidy path between the two events. That would be logical if the narrative were intended to be a kind of prophetic calendar of future world events (which is how many Christians in the past have tried to read it). It is clearly nothing of the kind, however. The visions come and go like scenes in a spectacular film. One vision is sometimes wrapped up in another one. From time to time, we leave a scene and then return to it later. Sometimes, what look like pictures of different events are in fact visions of the same event but from completely different perspectives. If we are looking for a tidy description of the future, we shall be disappointed, but if we are looking for a series of glimpses into the world of what we might call 'ultimate reality', then we shall be richly rewarded.

Those rich rewards don't require of the reader a degree in theology, or a thorough understanding of ancient literature or the Jewish spirituality of the first century. All that we really need are faith and imagination. Reading Revelation is like being led through a magnificent gallery of surrealist paintings, accompanied by a guide who occasionally interposes exactly the kind of comment we need to hear in order to understand what they mean. We shall never (at any rate, this side of heaven) understand every sentence of this amazing book, but that does not mean that we can't be open to and respond to its message.

It is a message that our generation, perhaps more than any that have preceded it, needs to hear. If the Christians of the first century were anxious about the future, so are we. If they felt helpless in the face of nameless powers, so do we. If they could not imagine what lay ahead for them or for their world, nor can we. The seven seals, seven trumpets and seven bowls of God's judgment are, we may well feel, about to be emptied on us, too.

One moment, our fear is of climate change; the next, it's terrorism; the next, it's pandemic disease or worldwide food shortage or massive computer failure or fraud, or some other malign and alien intrusion into the fragile complexity of our technological world. The great psychiatrist Carl Jung said that 'no one can live in peace in a house that he knows is shortly to tumble about his ears'. As we have already seen, there's a widespread anxiety that the whole house of our civilisation is looking distinctly shaky.

Our fears about disease and sickness thrive, despite astonishing advances in medical care, leading to a constantly rising life expectancy. Although societies in the developed world are incomparably the healthiest ever to have lived on this planet, far from being grateful or relieved, people worry about their health to an extraordinary degree. The media and an entire 'health and well-being' industry seek to convince us that the natural process of ageing can be avoided, longer life ensured and disease and death resisted if we are prepared to expend sufficient time and money on the effort.

These same societies also feel themselves exposed to dangers of war and especially terrorism, sometimes caused by a widespread disparity in wealth between the world's 'haves' and the world's 'have-nots' and sometimes the product of ideological fanaticism. This fear of terrorism surfaces from time to time, usually as the result of events near at hand. When it does, a widespread atmosphere of insecurity and even panic can result. Generally speaking, the 'enemy' is faceless, perhaps already living in the community, and possibly so consumed with hatred for all that the community stands for that he or she is prepared to sacrifice life itself to bring the whole edifice of prosperity crashing down. Who can forget the Twin Towers of New York on 11 September 2001? This in turn gives rise to xenophobia, the irrational fear of the alien, the stranger in the midst.

The third great fear in the developed world is environmental catastrophe, usually labelled 'global warming'. While debate rages over its causes (human activity or natural), its existence seems undeniable. Centuries-old glaciers melt, the ice caps of the planet begin to turn to water, drought strikes some regions and floods imperil others. The earth has, of course, experienced major climate changes at different times in its history, notably the ending of the last ice age, but, for the teeming billions who now inhabit the planet, such a change is a major threat to the survival, let alone prosperity, of the human race. For those who have become used to a relatively affluent lifestyle, it also raises doubts about our future comfort and security, and those of our children and grandchildren.

Of course, these concerns relate mostly to problems of prosperity and technology rather than of poverty and deprivation. They tend to centre on a range of issues that surface from time to time, disappear for a period (while we worry about something else) and then re-emerge.

The anxieties of the developing world are rather different. Some countries have been at the mercy of endless local conflicts and armed struggles, which have undermined attempts to improve agriculture or develop educational or medical programmes. In many areas of the world, the poorest people are also the most vulnerable to climate change, being dependent on the coming of monsoon or dry weather at the expected times. Harvests fail; hunger and then famine may follow. Time and again we have seen whole tracts of sub-Saharan Africa, for instance, reduced to dry desert or drowned in unseasonable floods, making impossible any hope of normal patterns of sowing, cultivation and harvesting. The poorest are also clearly the most vulnerable to natural disasters like earthquakes and typhoons.

At the same time, we have witnessed the deadly spread of the HIV/AIDS virus across huge areas of Africa, creating millions of orphans who may carry the virus in their own bloodstreams and in turn pass it on to their children.

The visions of Revelation vividly portray two worlds. In one of them, there is fear, terror, suffering and death. The fears of the developed world and those of the poorer nations are all represented in the vivid images described by John the Seer (so named because of all that he saw). In the other world of Revelation—the one portrayed in the frequent glimpses of the heavenly throne room of God—there is security, joy and love.

It has never been any part of the message of the scriptures to deny the reality of that first world, but they also bear eloquent witness to the reality of the second. In the end, they claim, in the fullness of God's purpose, the first world will fade away and the second one triumph. Revelation begins, as we have seen, with a vision of hope through the resurrection of Jesus, and it ends with a message of hope with the glory of the celestial city 'whose architect and builder is God' (Hebrews 11:10).

Meanwhile, the world as we know it is the world as it is, both harsh and lovely, brutal and beautiful. It is a world full of love and hate, kindness and cruelty, generosity and genocide. And it is that contrast, that astonishing amalgam of good and evil and its eventual consummation in the 'new Jerusalem', which the visions of Revelation set before the reader.

Key words in Revelation

In order to make much sense of the strange series of visions that make up most of the book of Revelation, we need, as well as a sanctified imagination, a few clues. Many of those clues are to be found in words or concepts that are foreign to us or that convey a different connotation now than they did to the first readers of this book of the Bible. So here is a kind of glossary of terms, designed to provide a key to unlocking some, at least, of the secrets of these visions.

Kingdom

Perhaps the key word in Revelation is 'kingdom'. The ancient world consisted of kingdoms—some of them vast empires, some tiny tribal enclaves. In each of them, however, there was someone who was the designated 'king' or 'emperor', and that person had absolute power. Where the king's writ ran, his word alone was law, and he exercised powers of life and death over his subjects. Consequently, the word 'kingdom' in the Bible carries the idea of an absolute rule. Although Greece had invented the notion of democracy, since the Roman Empire had been established democracy (certainly, as we understand it) had become largely an abstract concept. There was no doubt about who ruled the nations of the

Mediterranean area, including Greece, and that was the Roman Emperor. Senate and tribunes of the people could offer advice but, in the end, the decision always lay with him.

So when Revelation speaks of the 'kingdoms of this world', it is speaking of power over people exercised in an arbitrary manner. Sometimes such rule was benevolent and good; sometimes it was cruel and tyrannical. Forget modern notions of constitutional monarchy: a kingdom was the place where the king's will was done, for good or ill.

It is but a step from that knowledge to an understanding of what the biblical writers meant by the 'kingdom of God' or the 'kingdom of heaven'. These terms described a situation where God's will was done—something that Jesus urged his followers to pray for: 'Your kingdom come. Your will be done, on earth as it is in heaven' (Matthew 6:10). The kingdom of God is where his just and gentle rule is gladly accepted, where people live according to his standards of justice, righteousness and love. The kingdom of God already exists in heaven and, in an embryonic kind of way, wherever people on earth submit to his will. However, the world waits to see his kingdom extended to embrace every part of human society. That requires the submission of unruly human wills to the perfect will of God—a situation that, in the terms of these visions, is clearly 'not yet'.

Throne

A king sits on a throne. That may sound like a statement of the obvious but it is a vital part of the imagery of Revelation.

Constantly we are invited to see that there is a throne infinitely more powerful than any human one, and that its occupant's power is also infinite.

The throne stood in ancient times for power and for judgment. The one who sat on the throne had executive power. He or she could make things happen. The ruler spoke and the words turned into events: the command of God, 'Let there be light!' in the Genesis creation story, is a splendid example.

The one on the throne also had what we might call juridical power: he not only made the laws but also applied them. The king, or the king's representatives, applied the law and, in most premodern societies, the monarch was also the final point of appeal.

The throne in Revelation is awesome and majestic. Its first appearance in the visions (4:2–11) sets the scene. John, 'in the spirit', sees a throne in heaven with a figure seated on it—a figure who 'looked like' jasper and cornelian, crystalline rock-jewels that reflect light. The throne was surrounded by a rainbow of emerald colour. The rainbow, as we shall see, recurs frequently in Revelation as a constant reminder of the covenant that the Creator made with his creation after the flood—a covenant of faithful care (Genesis 9:13–16). All that follows, John is telling us, terrifying and awesome as it is, takes place under the arc of the rainbow, the sign of the eternal promise of mercy.

Like an earthly court, the monarch's throne is surrounded by the thrones of his ministers and lords, 24 of them. In this case, however, they are described as 'elders' (v. 4). 'Elder' here is the Greek word *presbyter*, which was the normal title of the presiding ministers in the local churches of the New Testament; it is, in fact, the root of our English word 'priest'. It was also used to describe the saints and patriarchs of Old Testament times. The elders are dressed in white robes and wear golden crowns.

As John looked, he saw that there were flashes of lightning, rumblings and peals of thunder emanating from the central throne, and in front of it burnt seven torches, 'which are the seven spirits of God'. In front of the throne he observed 'something like a sea of glass' (vv. 5–6).

Around the throne, and on each side of it, stood four living creatures, one with the appearance of a lion, one like an ox, one with a human face and one like a flying eagle. We can find their origins in the opening chapter of the prophet Ezekiel (1:1–11). They are probably meant to represent the whole of the living creation in its power, beauty, usefulness and God-given dignity.

This wonderful array of glorious creatures is engaged in endless worship of the One who is seated on the throne. The whole of creation—physical, animal and human—joins in the songs of praise, the elders 'casting down their golden crowns' before the throne, as Reginald Heber's hymn puts it ('Holy, holy, holy', 1826) recognising that their authority is devolved, not absolute. For absolute authority and power, our eyes are always drawn back to the central throne, because the One who sits there created all things and it is only by his will that they came into being and still exist (4:11).

This is a magnificent vision of splendour and power, mirroring in some way (but greatly excelling) that of the throne rooms of the Roman emperors. Here is the centre of cosmic power and also final judgment. As we shall now see, however, there is another figure in this heavenly throne room.

The Lamb

There is one figure, central to the whole story of Revelation, whose appearance is delayed until the next chapter. His description comes as something of a shock. Sharing the throne, we are told, is the figure of a Lamb, but this is no ordinary sheep—far from it. For one thing, he bears the marks of slaughter. This is a lamb that has been sacrificed. But he also has the hallmarks of divinity: 'seven horns and seven eyes... the seven spirits of God' (5:6).

As we shall see, this image is crucial to our understanding of the whole mysterious series of visions, for there, right at the heart of the place of cosmic power, is the sign of divine vulnerability. A lamb is weak, and a lamb that has been sacrificed is powerless: its work is done. Yet on the throne of the universe is this sacrificial Lamb, no longer dead but gloriously alive (as we saw in the opening vision of the whole book). Not only that, but the Lamb is stirred to 'wrath' by the signs of evil and suffering that afflict God's good creation (6:16). A vulnerable lamb and a wrathful one: the paradox is, at first sight, baffling. Yet this paradox is itself a profound clue to Revelation and one to which we shall often return.

Revelation deals with judgment and mercy, with the reality of evil and the means of redemption. No image expresses that contrast better than that of the Lamb, who is, of course, Jesus—identified clearly as such as the visions unfold.

Numbers

In apocalyptic writing, numbers are often very significant and carry hidden meanings. Seven, and its multiples, represent completeness. Two represents witness—the second confirming the first, so to speak. Four refers to creation, and twelve to the people of God (twelve tribes of Israel, twelve apostles of Christ). So 144,000 is especially significant, being twelve times twelve times a thousand, the 'complete' gathering of his people—not exclusive (as the Jehovah's Witnesses have thought) but inclusive of all.

There is a further use of numbers that tends to be completely baffling to readers today. It's called *gematria*, and it's a kind of numbers and letters game which makes it possible to refer cryptically to a person without using their name.

The best known example in Revelation is 666, 'the mark of the beast' (13:18), much beloved of horror film makers and spooky novelists. Numbers in the Greco-Roman and Jewish world were represented by alphabetic letters: there were no numerals, but each letter of the alphabet had a numerical value. We're familiar with the idea through 'Roman numerals', which are actually letters (M, C, X, L and so on). This meant that names could also be expressed as numbers. If the Greek form of the name Nero Caesar is written in Hebrew characters, its numerical value emerges as 666, but if the Greek word for 'beast' is expressed in Hebrew, it also emerges as 666. So it's possible for the writer of Revelation to identify Nero with the 'beast' in chapter 13 without actually saying so, as readers and hearers would probably be able to decode the message for themselves.

Angels

One problem for today's reader of Revelation is the multiplicity of 'angels', not all of them the good and beneficent beings that we usually associate with the title. On the one hand, there are the familiar angels who do God's bidding—his 'messengers' who bear both blessing and judgment to the earth in his name. On the other hand, there are also 'angels' who fight against God and are eventually expelled from the heavenly stage on which this cosmic drama is acted out.

Revelation seems to reflect a later Jewish understanding of the role of angels, probably dating from post-exilic times. We have a vivid, if strange, example of it in the story that sets the scene for the whole book of Job: 'One day the heavenly beings came to present themselves before the Lord, and Satan also came among them' (Job 1:6). 'Satan' means 'adversary' or 'accuser', and that is certainly his role in this instance: he is evidently not the beneficent kind of figure that we normally associate with angels. The title 'angel' literally means 'messenger', and the Bible generally sees them as God's emissaries, conveying to human beings messages of warning or encouragement and doing God's will. However, Jesus spoke of 'the devil and his angels' (Matthew 25:41) and in Revelation we also see them in action.

These rival hierarchies of spirits are seen as ranged on opposing sides, God's angels in conflict with Satan's angels. We may legitimately see this as a vivid and memorable way of depicting the reality of the 'battle' between the will of God and the will of his adversaries, in whatever form or personification they may present themselves.

This concept of a cosmic struggle between the forces of good and evil needs to be distinguished from the metaphysical system called 'dualism', in which good and evil are seen as equally powerful and ever-present forces in the universe. Revelation is quite clear about who sits on the throne and who doesn't.

Heaven

It may seem surprising that as fundamental a concept as 'heaven' needs to be interpreted where the book of Revelation and its message is concerned. Heaven, to us, is where God is—a place of perfect holiness, peace and joy. It's where we hope to go one day, to join all the saints of God. That is heaven as it's popularly understood, and that picture of heaven can certainly be traced in the pages of the New Testament and the language of Christian hymnody, prayer and devotion.

Heaven as Revelation reveals it in its earlier visions doesn't seem exactly to match that picture, however. John 'looked' and 'in heaven a door stood open' (4:1). He was told that if he came near, he would be shown 'what must take place after this'. So he was given a glimpse into the world of the infinite, as though the curtains had been drawn back on a cosmic stage, on which the unseen but real conflict between light and darkness was being played out. God was there, as we have seen, and he was joined on his throne by Jesus, the Lamb. God's people were there, too, from 'every tribe and language and people and nation' (5:9).

However, it soon becomes clear that, on this cosmic stage, other and more sinister forces are also present. The Lamb opens the 'seven seals' and there emerge, one by one, four deadly horsemen, representing the four most common plagues and perils of earthly life: military power and conquest, war and slaughter, famine, and death by pestilence (6:1–8). John hears voices appealing to God to judge and avenge the injustices being done on the earth, and a cataclysmic vision of God's final judgment follows, before which even the most powerful rulers and magnates cower in fear (vv. 9–17).

Can this really be heaven, the place of ultimate peace and justice? Surely not, as we have usually understood it. Yet if we think of heaven as the place where truth is revealed, a realm of spiritual reality far removed from fantasy and wish fulfilment, then these visions tell us that God and Jesus and heaven are not unaffected by the cruel and unjust events that take place on earth, just as those events are not unaffected by what happens in heaven. We do not live in a dualistic universe, where good and evil, religion and real life are disconnected, but in a universe where they are bound up in a greater truth, which is the final purpose of God. Revelation ends, as we shall see, in the coming together of earthly experience and heavenly purpose in the eventual triumph of God over all that is evil, cruel, exploitative and unjust. Finally we have heaven as we understand it.

This may all seem rather abstract and complicated, but, as we make our way through the visions that John records, we shall see that they present a single and essentially quite straightforward message. At the moment, we may feel like adding our voices to those calling on God to 'do something now'. The evidence of human suffering, injustice and pain is all around us and it is natural for us to question why a good and loving God appears either powerless or unwilling to intervene. John's visions do not offer easy answers to such questions but they do face them head-on. The 'open door' that he sees offers a different perspective on the most profound issues of good and evil, power and weakness, human choice and divine will, and this is the perspective that we need if we are to make any kind of sense of the world we live in now and the future that God has purposed for humanity. The unfolding of that perspective is the story of the book of Revelation.

Starting with the churches...

Revelation 2–3

John is given 'letters' to be written to seven Christian churches in Asia. They are messages of encouragement, correction or warning, addressed to Christians facing opposition and the threat of persecution.

'And to the angel of the church in Laodicea write: The words of the Amen, the faithful and true witness, the origin of God's creation:

'I know your works; you are neither cold nor hot. I wish that you were either cold or hot. So, because you are lukewarm, and neither cold nor hot, I am about to spit you out of my mouth. For you say, 'I am rich, I have prospered, and I need nothing.' You do not realize that you are wretched, pitiable, poor, blind, and naked. Therefore I counsel you to buy from me gold refined by fire so that you may be rich; and white robes to clothe you and to keep the shame of your nakedness from being seen; and salve to anoint your eyes so that you may see. I reprove and discipline those whom I love. Be earnest, therefore, and repent. Listen! I am standing at the door, knocking; if you hear my voice and open the door, I will come in to you and

eat with you, and you with me. To the one who conquers I will give a place with me on my throne, just as I myself conquered and sat down with my Father on his throne. Let anyone who has an ear listen to what the Spirit is saying to the churches.'
REVELATION 3:14–22

As we have seen, Revelation began with the vision of the risen Christ (1:10–20), his assurance of victory over death and the grave setting the tone for the whole book. We do not move at once to the heavenly scene or the cosmic stage that will feature later throughout its pages, but to the churches in seven towns in the region we now call Turkey. In other words, before we are invited to look at visions of the security and glory of heaven or the sufferings of the world and its people, we are taken to ground level, to the ordinary, very human communities of Christians to whom the message of this book is primarily addressed. They will see, and so shall we, amazing sights. Heaven will be opened to their gaze. Saints and angels will sing and prayers will rise like incense. At the same time, in an alternating series of scenes, they will see horror, devastation, suffering and judgment. Some of that suffering is through what we call 'natural' disaster, some is the result of human sin and greed and some the work, it seems, of malign spiritual forces, enemies of God. All of this culminates in the great moment of judgment, when 'Babylon the great' (17:5), the epitome of everything that sets itself up against God and his people, is brought low.

The visions that follow are played out on a stage that is not limited by space, time, geography or history. The truths that they reflect are essentially timeless or eternal. So why does the book open with actual places, towns on a human map, at specific dates in human history? And what might the answer to that question tell us about the role of the Christian Church, then and now, in the vast unfolding purposes of God?

If the book of Revelation is engaged in a search for the answer to profound questions about evil and suffering and their place in a world created by a loving God, do those little communities of faith in the first century, or the worldwide community of faith that struggles to follow Christ in the 21st, contribute anything to that answer? The fact that the visions seen by John begin with these messages of Jesus to seven actual churches suggests that they do, perhaps because, unless the answer makes sense at street level, it's not likely to make sense anywhere else.

Saints and martyrs feature throughout the visions of Revelation, but they are always seen around the throne of God, rather than engaged in the business of living out the heavenly visions down on earth. Yet that is where the immediate challenge lies for us. However confident we might be about the reality of eventual heavenly bliss (or however strange and elusive that prospect might seem to us), it is here and now that we have to engage with the fears, doubts and anxieties of everyday life. It makes sense that this book of heavenly visions starts, as surely it must, with the harsh reality of ordinary life for the members of the churches in those seven Asian towns. They were not all the churches in the region, by any means; perhaps they were the ones John knew personally, or simply representatives of the whole. At this period, they were certainly 'young' churches, many of them planted by the missionary work of Paul and his associates 30 years or so earlier. It is to them, or their 'angels' (whoever they may be—no one seems to know for sure), that the first series of messages is addressed.

At the time, the cult of emperor worship was strong in the area, and growing, and followers of Christ were increasingly being seen as non-conformist, awkward, idiosyncratic. They refused to accord to a human being, however eminent, the worship that was uniquely due to God. Rome, however, liked things neat, tidy and orderly. Those who stood out could expect harsh treatment.

We may feel, in an increasingly secularised West, that today's Church faces similar pressures. Christians are often seen as awkward, odd or simply troublemakers. Why can't they just conform to the majority view, 'live and let live', stop being obstructive in the face of such things as sexual 'liberation', materialism, abortion on demand, crude and abusive humour and so on? No one objects to churches and Christians who quietly go with the flow but, when they insist on trying to turn the tide, attitudes change. Then they are likely to be labelled narrow-minded bigots or killjoys. In different details but very similar circumstances, the seven churches of Asia faced the same kind of opposition—though potentially (and actually, in some places) physically much more threatening.

The 'messages' of Revelation 2 and 3 are rather like the kind of inspection reports that hospitals and schools get today. Each message includes some words of commendation about what is good in the church, and in all but two of them there are also quite serious warnings about areas of failure. In one or two cases, unless matters improve, they are warned, they may be put under 'special measures' (as OFSTED puts it) or even shut down completely.

The first message (2:1–7) is to the church at Ephesus, a large and influential city in the province and a well-established centre of Roman religion. The Christian message was preached there by Paul and his associates and a strong church was founded. Notable members included Priscilla and Aquila, and, according to tradition, at some stage the apostle John and the mother of Jesus lived there.

On the whole, Ephesus gets praise. Its members have been patient and endured opposition, 'bearing up' (v. 3) for the sake of the name of Christ. The main criticism of the church, however, is that it has lost 'the love [it] had at first' (v. 4). That lost love is so vital to its health and well-being that recapturing it is seen as essential to the church's survival. Without love, the church will die: its 'lampstand' will be removed from its place (v. 5). Even beleaguered Christians, resisting the pressures of the culture surrounding them, need to practise love. Loveless protest is doomed to failure.

The second of the seven churches to receive a message is the one at Smyrna (vv. 8–11), on the western coast of the province: it's now called Izmir. The city had been splendidly rebuilt after being largely destroyed during a war in the third century BC and was full of grand buildings, many of them erected to honour the emperor. Smyrna was rich and a centre of emperor worship, but the church was persecuted and poor.

Along with Philadelphia, Smyrna is one of the two churches to get what we might call a perfect report. Although its members are financially poor, in everything that matters they are rich. They have stood firm against two powerful opponents—the emperor cult and a group described as false Jews: they 'say that they are Jews and are not' (v. 9). The latter reference may relate to an exemption from participation in the cult of emperor worship, which Jews had gained but which was denied to Christians, although many of them still claimed to be, and were by birth, Jewish. The Jews in Smyrna, clearly, were not in favour of extending this exemption to Jewish Christians. The persecution faced by the church in Smyrna will inevitably last for a time, they are told. But if they are 'faithful until death', they will be given 'the crown of life' (v. 10). For this reason, they should not fear. Christ knows what they are undergoing and his Spirit is with them.

The third message is for the church at Pergamum (vv. 12–17), the provincial capital and a centre not only for the worship of Zeus but also for their 'local' god, Asklepios, who was credited with healing miracles at his shrine in the city. Pergamum had a massive temple to Zeus and it was also a prime centre of emperor worship, with yet another temple dedicated to the current emperor, Domitian: 'Satan's throne' is how the message describes it. Pergamum, in other words, was the headquarters of the opposition!

One of the recurring phrases in these messages to the churches is 'I know'. The Lord knows what his people are going through; he knows their fears and anxieties, their weaknesses and their strengths. That is, in itself, an enormous encouragement. It is always disabling to feel that no one knows or understands our situation or how we feel. 'I know,' the Lord says, 'where you are living, where Satan's throne is. Yet you are holding fast to my name, and you did not deny your faith in me even in the days of Antipas my witness, my

faithful one, who was killed among you, where Satan lives'
(v. 13).

All the same, there is a criticism—not of the majority of
the church, but of some members who have been led astray
by paganism. Perhaps out of fear, or simply in order to avoid
unwelcome attention, they have gone along with some
aspects of the local religious practice. Perhaps they have
nodded towards emperor worship—a pinch of incense at
the shrine—or attended a ceremony at one of the temples. It
may all have seemed harmless enough, but here it is likened
to 'the teaching of Balaam' (Numbers 31:16), who led the
Israelites into compromise with paganism. The message is
stern: 'Repent then', or those who have failed in this way will
be judged by 'the sword of my mouth'—the words of God
(v. 16).

The next church to receive a message is Thyatira (vv.
18–29). Again, many good things are noted. The church is
growing; there are signs of spiritual blessing; there is love
and faith. There are, however, two negatives. First, they are
tolerating a woman prophet dubbed 'Jezebel'—presumably
after the notorious queen who worshipped Baal and opposed
Elijah (1 Kings 18:19). Instead of listening to her, they should
be shunning her and her influence in the church. She seems
to have been encouraging them to eat food that had been
offered in sacrifice to heathen gods (a practice discussed, in
rather less trenchant language, by Paul in his letter to the
Corinthian church: 1 Corinthians 8).

Thyatira's second failing concerns what the message calls
'fornication' (v. 20). This may literally mean sexual promis-
cuity or it may refer simply to flirting with pagan practices

or institutions. The Christians are to keep clear of every appearance of evil—as, the message agrees, most of them have done. The reward for faithfulness will be 'authority' (v. 26) and to be a guiding light ('morning star': v. 28) to the nations, the Gentiles.

Sardis is the next church to be addressed (3:1–6). This city was once the home of King Croesus (celebrated in the saying 'rich as Croesus') and shared in his affluence, but now it has become poor, and so have the Christians. Their poverty is not just financial. 'I know your works,' says the Lord; 'you have a name for being alive, but you are dead' (v. 1). This is the most crushing criticism of any of the churches, only slightly softened by the observation that there were still 'a few people in Sardis who have not soiled their clothes' (v. 4). The call is to repentance, and, as usual, a generous promise is given: if they do repent, they will be restored, dressed in white robes and confessed by Jesus before his Father.

The church at Philadelphia, by contrast, gets a near-perfect report (vv. 7–13). Although poor ('you have but little power'), they have kept Christ's word and not denied his name. Because they have shown 'patient endurance', he will keep them in 'the hour of trial'. They now face an 'open door', which no one can shut. Great possibilities lie ahead. If they remain faithful, they will become 'a pillar in the temple of my God' (v. 12), citizens of the heavenly Jerusalem.

From faithful Philadelphia we turn to the final message, to the desperately confused church at Laodicea (vv. 14–22). They think they are rich and prosperous; they are self-satisfied, not aware of any need. That kind of spiritual complacency is always dangerous. For the Christians at Laodicea, it has bred a blindness to their real needs. In fact, they are 'wretched, pitiable, poor, blind, and naked' (v. 17). Their faith is neither hot nor cold, just lukewarm, and that is worse than useless. It is the curse of 'respectable' religion that it can become something we take for granted—routine rather than life-enhancing, complacent rather than committed.

If they want true riches, they should recognise their plight and seek true spiritual riches, which Christ will gladly supply: 'gold refined by fire so that you may be rich; and white robes to clothe you and to keep the shame of your nakedness from being seen; and salve to anoint your eyes so that you may see' (v. 18).

However, as in all the words of challenge and correction, there are also words of encouragement for Laodicea. The Lord only disciplines and reproves those he loves (v. 19). Then there follows probably the best-known verse in the whole of Revelation: 'Listen! I am standing at the door, knocking; if you hear my voice and open the door, I will come in to you and eat with you, and you with me' (v. 20).

Many people associate this verse with Holman Hunt's famous painting *The Light of the World*, which pictures Jesus, lamp in hand and crown of thorns on his brow, knocking on a closed door that is covered in creepers and brambles. Usually we apply it to the individual, taking it as an invitation to 'open our life' to Jesus and welcome him in. Here in Revelation, of course, the words are addressed not to an individual but to a church—a church that has lost its way and become lukewarm in its faith, deluding itself that it's all right when in fact it is spiritually dead. The church has changed, but Jesus has not. He is the same as ever, and his invitation is the same. Churches and individuals may deliberately or unwittingly exclude Jesus, but he is still waiting 'at the door', wanting simply to be invited back in.

The messages end with an invitation that echoes the words of Jesus at the end of many of his parables: 'Let anyone who has an ear listen to what the Spirit is saying to the churches' (v. 22).

Assuming we have that 'ear', what exactly do we hear from the messages to those churches of long ago? First of all, surely, that nothing changes very much: churches today have many of the same problems. Most of us don't experience the direct persecution that some of those first-century Christians were facing or knew that they were about to face. On the other hand, we have to contend with a sceptical and sometimes intolerant secularism that would have been completely foreign to their experience. They lived in an intensely religious world. The only question people faced was 'Which religion?' It's true that there were groups like the Stoics (Acts 17:18), who held views fairly similar to those of modern Humanists, but they were not rejecting any and every notion of religious faith. Their philosophy was of the present, holding out no hope of future life beyond death—much like the Jewish Sadducees.

We face today a militant atheism that campaigns against every kind of religious faith, believing it to be a superstitious throwback to days of ignorance and fear. It may be that the coming years will see such views strengthen—even, perhaps, become the accepted culture. Then Christians and people of other religious faiths will be a minority once again, rejected and even reviled by their fellow citizens. We shall then feel much like the Christians at Pergamum.

More immediately, we face the challenge of compromise (like Thyatira), a reluctance to swim against the tide or stand up for what we know to be right. In other cases, the lack may be of love, like the church at Ephesus: something has died in the heart of the church and it has become loveless. When that happens, it loses its chief distinguishing attribute. Then there is the problem of the church at Sardis: an unfulfilled church, with a reputation for life but, in reality, spiritually dead.

Perhaps worst of all is Laodicea, the lukewarm church. Not only then, but equally now, the times demand churches that are not lukewarm but on fire with the life of the Spirit.

Yet the final picture of these messages is wonderfully encouraging. The Lord of the Church stands at the door of the Church, knocking. He hasn't given up on her. The door can be opened and the Saviour can come in and restore what has been lost. As the story moves on and the visions of spiritual warfare unfold, we shall be reminded again and again that, although the Lamb shares the heavenly throne, his heart is still with his people on earth.

Facing our fears:
why do the innocent suffer?

Revelation 4—9

These chapters begin with visions of the glory of heaven—the throne of God, 'four living creatures' and Jesus, 'the Lamb', who is also called 'the Lion of the tribe of Judah, the Root of David'. Placed among these visions of glory is a series of visions of catastrophes: the four deadly horsemen, hail, earthquake, pollution, darkness, plague and locusts. Through it all, the saints remain saintly but the evil do not repent.

And I saw the seven angels who stand before God, and seven trumpets were given to them. Another angel with a golden censer came and stood at the altar; he was given a great quantity of incense to offer with the prayers of all the saints on the golden altar that is before the throne. And the smoke of the incense, with the prayers of the saints, rose before God from the hand of the angel. Then the angel took the censer and filled it with fire from the altar and threw it on the earth; and there were peals of thunder, rumblings, flashes of lightning, and an earthquake.
REVELATION 8:2–5

It's absolutely typical of Revelation—but also, if you think about it, of the whole business of dreams and visions—that after the letters to the churches, and hot on the heels of two visions of utter peace and joy in chapters 4 and 5, the scene instantly changes. At the end of chapter 5 there is a sublime picture of pure heavenly worship: 'To the one seated on the throne and to the Lamb be blessing and honour and glory and might...' (v. 13). What immediately follows? The Lamb opens four of the seven seals of a parchment scroll with which he has been entrusted and the 'four horsemen of the Apocalypse', as they are known, come charging on to the scene. (6:1–8).

The horses are of different colours, each one with its rider representing a different plague or peril that afflicts the human race. The first horse (white) with its rider represents the conqueror, a common foe in the ancient world, where kings and their armies would attack and subdue a neighbouring nation and take away its fittest and ablest people as slaves. Today this horseman perhaps represents the subjugation of societies, tribes and peoples by powerful regimes—the kind of fate suffered for many decades by the people of southern Sudan, for instance, or in the apartheid era by black people in South Africa.

The second horse is 'bright red' (v. 4), or perhaps we could say 'blood red', for it represents war. Its rider 'was permitted to take peace from the earth'. As a result, 'people would slaughter one another'. One of the greatest triumphs of this horseman must be the vast military cemeteries of northern France and Belgium, with their graves of soldiers who fell in their millions in the endless muddy battles of the First World

War. Every human generation, however, has encountered the second horseman of the Apocalypse.

The third horse is black. Its sinister rider represents famine: 'a quart of wheat for a day's pay' (v. 6). We might paraphrase this as 'a loaf of bread for £35'. The horseman carries scales, but they are the balances of injustice, for the rich will survive (hence 'the olive oil and the wine' remain undamaged) while the poor starve.

The fourth horse is pale green in colour and represents death in its most sudden forms: sword, famine, pestilence and by the jaws of 'wild animals of the earth' (v. 8). Our modern equivalents would be, I suppose, terrorist bombs, pandemic disease, air and road accidents and violent crime.

The rest of chapter 6 describes the opening of the fifth and sixth seals by the Lamb. The fifth seal represents martyrdom —those who had been 'slaughtered for the word of God and for the testimony they had given' (v. 9). Each one is given a white robe and 'told to rest a little longer' until the ranks of the martyrs are complete.

The sixth seal represents a terrible earthquake, so catastrophic that everyone, rich and poor, kings and magnates, generals and nobodies, hides in caves from its effects. So appalling is its impact that another angel is sent with 'the seal of the living God' to order that the destruction should be held back until the servants of God are marked 'with a seal on their foreheads' (7:2–3).

This introduces a pause in the sequence of calamities, followed by another heavenly vision. Yet again, the horror is countered with the assurance that the One seated on the heavenly throne and the Lamb beside him have not lost control. The saints and martyrs stand around the throne of God and an 'elder' promises that 'the Lamb at the centre of the throne will be their shepherd, and he will guide them to springs of the water of life' (v. 17). God himself will 'wipe away every tear from their eyes' (v. 18), a beautiful echo of a prophecy of Isaiah (25:8). It is a vision of divine comfort, peace and security.

What then follows? The Lamb opens the seventh seal. For 'half an hour' there is 'silence in heaven' (a lovely touch: 8:1). Then the seven angels who stand before God assemble with their seven trumpets, the cries of the saints and martyrs for justice rise like incense from a censer, the censer is hurled by an angel on to the earth—and mayhem follows! The gentle, comforting Lamb has changed: now we see 'the wrath of the Lamb', which was spoken of at the end of the previous vision of heaven (6:16), the most gentle of creatures becoming a symbol of righteous anger and judgment.

The first angel brings 'hail and fire' (8:7) that burns up a third of the land, a third of the trees and a third of the green grass. The second angel throws a burning mountain into the sea, which then turns to 'blood' (v. 9), and a third of all sea creatures die and a third of the ships are destroyed. The third angel causes a star, called 'Wormwood', to fall from heaven into the waters and rivers of the earth, which become polluted (v. 11).

When the fourth angel blows his trumpet, a third of the sun is 'struck' (v. 12), followed by a third of the moon and a third of the stars, so that light is darkened everywhere. The fifth angel carries the key to a 'bottomless pit' (9:1) from which, when he opens it, noxious fumes arise. Weird creatures swarm from the pit—locusts with bodies like horses and human faces, whose bite is painful but not fatal. Only those who bear 'the seal of God on their foreheads' are spared (v. 4). This particular affliction has a time limit of five months.

The sixth angel blows his trumpet and the earth is stricken with 'fire and smoke and sulphur' (v. 18) from the mouths of the horses of a vast cavalry. Despite this, John records, the people of earth do not repent but continue 'worshipping demons and idols', and indulging in 'sorceries', 'fornication' and 'thefts' (vv. 20–21).

There is no doubt that these visions are the stuff of nightmares, but, as part of a divine revelation, they must have been recorded for a deeper reason than simply to scare us. Three of the four horsemen of chapter 6 represent evils for which human sin could be held at least partly responsible: war, conquest and famine. The subsequent disasters, however, are related to the creation itself, to events over which humans have little or no control. If, as has already been suggested, Revelation was written around the time of the eruption of Vesuvius, which caused such enormous destruction and loss of life, these visions were possibly intended to speak to people who were fearful of what might come next: noxious fumes, earthquakes, darkness, the destruction of the fields and the pollution of the sea. Quite apart from specific historical events, the people of the Mediterranean area were familiar with erupting volcanoes: Etna could match Vesuvius for terror.

Fear is the natural response to such terrifying natural phenomena, but a more positive response is awe—to recognise that the creation is greater than we are, that wind, wave, lightning and thunder (terrifying as they may be) are part of the environment in which the Creator has set us. Awe leads, these visions suggest, to repentance, which is simply another way of saying conversion of heart. Sadly, the survivors in chapter 9 experience the terror but miss the awe: when the trouble has passed and the storm died down, they breathe a sigh of relief and resume the lives they were living before. However, that is not the end of the story, for them or for us.

Yet again the scene dramatically changes. A 'mighty angel' appears in the vision, 'wrapped in a cloud, with a rainbow over his head' (10:1). Suddenly, with the swiftness of the blink of an eye, tragedy turns to triumph, judgment to covenant mercy. At this point (to which we shall return), we move on to what many scholars would see as the key chapters of the whole book.

In the coming chapters, we are invited to face the realities of human suffering and distress so vividly portrayed in the visions that John the seer has just experienced. The contrast between scenes of beauty, peace and mercy on the one hand, and grotesque images of human suffering on the other, is no more than a reflection of the reality of human existence. We have love and compassion alongside brutality and violence. We have the joy of birth alongside the sadness of bereavement. In the natural world, the world created by our loving God, we have streams of life-giving water and the refreshment of cool breezes alongside earthquakes, volcanic eruptions and drought.

This is not an argument from theory but the observation of daily experience. We have an accident in the car and the people who come to our help are caring, kind and thoughtful, but we go into the supermarket and someone steals our handbag. The busy bee that pollinates our fruit can also sting us painfully, and, for some people, that sting can lead to serious complications and even death. The harmless brook in which we dabble our feet on holiday can become a raging torrent at times, flooding homes in the village below. We can't avoid the fact that we live in a risky world, a world where pleasure and pain, peace and conflict, life and death are ever present. The priest-scientist John Polkinghorne entitled his book on this subject *The Way the World Is*, a concept of profound simplicity.

This is the world as the visions of Revelation reflect it. Like contrasting scenes in a film, the whole story flickers before our eyes on the cosmic stage that John calls heaven, the place of ultimate reality. The four horsemen are part of that reality: conflict, war, famine and plague. But so is the heavenly throne room; so are the praises of the saints; so is the promise that God will wipe away every tear from sorrowing eyes.

It is not a matter of choosing one or the other scenario of life. This is life as it is, on a planet subject to physical traumas that are part of its pattern of existence, and in a world inhabited by people who, by the will of their Creator, are given the terrible freedom to choose their own way. Eventually, Revelation tells us, it will not be like this, but for now we must live in the only world we have and trust that its destiny is in the hands of its Creator, who is loving and not malign.

Of course, we can't escape the fact that Revelation sees war, conflict, famine and plague in terms of judgment. The various angels are agents of God's judgment: their trumpet calls signal that the courts of highest heaven are declaring judgment on what is evil and corrupt in God's world. But judgment, in the language of the New Testament, is not simply a matter of arbitrary vengeance or even divine retribution. The Greek word used in Revelation is more subtle than that. It carries various overtones: separation (its basic meaning), decision, resolution and determination. It is the inevitable consequence of choices, the demonstration that actions have reactions, but it is also the process by which good is separated or distinguished from that which is evil. In the end, God's creation must be purged of anything that corrupts it, like removing rotten apples from a barrel. His patience is inexhaustible (Micah 2:7)—which is why the observation is so pertinent that even after all the warnings and horrors, the people 'did not repent' (Revelation 9:21).

However, that raises another problem for today's reader of Revelation. Surely many of the horrors and disasters that afflict the human race are accidental and arbitrary, not specific and discriminatory? How, then, can they be seen to urge us to repentance? The clearly innocent suffer as much as, and often more than, those we would deem guilty. Children die in natural disasters or pandemics; agents of mercy are as likely to hit a roadside bomb as a squad of terrorists. In that case, how can such disasters be seen as judgment? Are they not, as we have already observed, simply the way the world is?

It is true that to the mind of the Hebrew scriptures (the Old Testament) everything that happens, good or bad, is in some sense the 'will of God'. Because he is Yahweh, the I AM, the God of creation and life, then everything that happens must take place under his ultimate control or permission. Thus, famine, plague, war and pestilence are in some way under his authority—and so are sunshine, the early and late rains, and the life of the seed in the ground. It is but an incautious step from this to a cause-and-effect view of God, who could be seen as simply manipulating people, events and history itself like so many pieces on a cosmic chess board.

It would seem that Jesus did not, however, entirely accept this cause-and-effect view of God's relationship to his creation. Some bystanders had raised the subject of certain Galileans who had been killed by Pilate's officers while they were making their sacrifices. Jesus asked whether they therefore assumed that these people were worse sinners than all the other Galileans who had escaped such a fate. He then made his own reference to an event that was obviously in the news at the time. A tower in Siloam had collapsed, falling on 18 unfortunate people and killing them. Did the bystanders think, he asked, that those 18 were worse offenders than everybody else in Jerusalem? (Luke 13:1–5). Whatever they thought, Jesus simply answered 'No' to both questions, while going on to warn, in a general sense, that God calls for repentance from everyone. This had been part of his message from the very start of his ministry: 'Repent, and believe in the good news' (Mark 1:15).

We are not pawns on a chess board but self-conscious, morally responsible creatures, who make real decisions about our choices and actions. If we were less than that, we would be moral robots, simply moving about and doing what we were told to do by a heavenly orchestrator. That would not be the God of the Bible, who, right from the beginning, gave his human children the fearful right to choose. Much of what we suffer in life is indeed the consequence of human choices, ours and other people's—the 'fallenness' that flows from disobedience. There remains, though, the significant matter of natural disasters, accidents and diseases, which happen, it seems, in a random kind of way.

Both of these kinds of problems, these agents or incidences of human suffering, are pictured in the images of Revelation. Some, like war, the misuse of power and famine caused by human greed, clearly fall into the category of self-inflicted wounds. Others, like plague, accident and famine caused by drought, can be seen as random events, not the fault of human choice (though sometimes exacerbated by it). The message of the visions is the same in both cases, in fact: God has not been taken by surprise; his creation has not gone into freefall; he is still in ultimate control of what is happening. Those who are responsible for the suffering and pain of others must answer to him for their actions. The innocent who suffer will have their tears wiped away. Neither type of person is hidden from the God who is both Creator and Redeemer. That is the meaning of the constantly returning imagery of the throne in heaven: it's not empty!

As we shall see as we turn now to the central and critical visions of Revelation, the bittersweet nature of human history and experience is neither a denial of God's authority nor the last word about human destiny. Indeed, it is the mystery that is the heart of the Christian gospel.

The cosmic conflict

Revelation 10–11

In these chapters, the heart of Revelation, the final confrontation between the powers of worldly evil and the divine purpose of God is enacted in a series of visions. The reporter, John, is given a scroll and told to eat it. It is both bitter and sweet, as is the gradual unfolding of the mystery of evil and the promise of its eventual defeat.

And I saw another mighty angel coming down from heaven, wrapped in a cloud, with a rainbow over his head; his face was like the sun, and his legs like pillars of fire. He held a little scroll open in his hand… Then the voice that I had heard from heaven spoke to me again, saying, 'Go, take the scroll that is open in the hand of the angel who is standing on the sea and on the land.' So I went to the angel and told him to give me the little scroll; and he said to me, 'Take it, and eat; it will be bitter to your stomach, but sweet as honey in your mouth.' … Then the seventh angel blew his trumpet, and there were loud voices in heaven, saying, 'The kingdom of the world has become the kingdom of our Lord and of his Messiah, and he will reign forever and ever.'

REVELATION 10:1, 8–9; 11:15

So far, Revelation has offered us a series of contrasting visions, alternating between scenes of the heavenly throne room and an unfolding panorama of human suffering and distress. What we await—as, it seems, does John himself, pictured as a kind of involved observer—is some kind of explanation or interpretation of their message. We could well feel that, in one sense, we already know the situation they are depicting. We assume, as the poet Robert Browning said, that 'God's in his heaven' and that it's all very secure and confident there, and we are well aware from our own daily experience that on earth there is a constant amalgam of joy and suffering. What we long for is some clue to make sense of the contrast, to know that it is not simply a pointless confusion or grotesque power game played by a cruel and arbitrary god rather than a loving Creator. One character in Shakespeare's *King Lear* says, 'As flies to wanton boys are we to the gods—they kill us for their sport', and that is certainly how life has seemed to many people.

Now, however, the time has come for the mystery to be solved. Now at last the heavenly presenters (angelic figures, for the most part) are to unfold the 'secret' that will make sense of both the security of heaven and the insecurities of earth. 'Mystery' in biblical language does not mean, as it does in everyday speech, something that we can't understand, but simply something that needs to be revealed. A 'mystery', in that sense, is not without meaning, but its meaning needs to be unfolded or made clear to us. For Paul, the whole gospel of Jesus is a 'mystery' because it can only be received by revelation (Ephesians 3:2–6).

The pattern employed throughout Revelation is apparent

in these passages. Always, the good news precedes the bad. The visions of the heavenly throne room, with their assurance that the One who sits on the throne is in ultimate control, fill the cosmic stage. Before we see the ugly truth about the presence and power of evil, we will be reminded of the ultimate triumph of all that is good. There will be, the observer is told, no more delay: 'the mystery of God will be fulfilled' (10:7). This is it!

So we see the angel (adorned, we note, with the 'rainbow' of the covenant mercy of God) holding the scroll, which is offered to the observer. John is told to take it and eat it, but is warned that while it will be sweet as honey in the mouth, when it reaches the stomach it will be bitter. He does what he is told, and finds that it is indeed both sweet and bitter. There is an echo here of the prophet Ezekiel, who was also told to eat a scroll. In his case, all he experienced was the sweetness of its taste in his mouth (Ezekiel 3:3), but his later experiences proved that the consequence of bearing testimony to uncomfortable truths would be bitter indeed.

Why, we may ask, is the message of the scroll in Revelation both sweet and bitter? We have already seen how true the imagery is to human experience. Everyone knows that life is both bitter and sweet. Love and hate, joy and pain, truth and lies, peace and war, security and danger mark our daily path. To pretend that it is not so is simply to close our eyes to the facts of existence.

Now, in this vision, we will learn that this very contrast—paradox, really—is at the heart of the message of the gospel itself. Far from being a problem, as it is often presented, it is the solution, the answer to the mystery. Before we get there, however, several dramatic and terrible scenes must be enacted on the cosmic stage.

It's fascinating to see the way in which the observer John is constantly drawn into the visions, actually becoming part of them. For me, this enhances the dreamlike quality of the whole narrative, because sometimes we find ourselves taking part in our own dreams and nightmares and at other times we seem to be simply watching other people and remote events.

Now, in chapter 11, John is told to take a measuring rod and measure the inner court of the temple. Significantly, he is not told to measure the whole site, including the outer courts. His task is only to check the dimensions of the inner courts—the courts of women and of men and the Holy Place. These, he is told, will be preserved in the coming destruction of both the temple and the holy city, Jerusalem.

In fact, by the time the book of Revelation was written, both of those events had almost certainly already taken place. In AD70 there was a Jewish uprising against the Romans. It was eventually put down, with great loss of life, and the Romans exacted revenge by destroying the temple and much of the city of Jerusalem. Many Jews fled the scene, marking the start of the mass dispersion that saw Jewish communities taking root in many countries in Europe and the Middle East.

The promise here in Revelation 11 is that even in a time of such calamity, God will preserve the heart of true religion, the inner sanctuary. As a matter of historical fact, the whole of the temple was destroyed, including the inner courts, but that does not affect the essential message of this vision. Here, the language is not about preserving the relics of the old temple but about guarding the essential heart of the new one. As we can see from the letter to the Hebrews, the old temple and its priesthood and sacrifices had been superseded by a new spiritual temple, the Church, and a new and great 'high priest', Jesus, the Son of God (Hebrews 4:14). For the apostles and their successors, this Church was the 'new Israel' and they, Jews and Gentiles together, were the people of the new covenant that Christ sealed in his blood (1 Corinthians 11:25).

Although the temple was destroyed, the vision holds true, because the spiritual inner court, the heart of true worship and the meeting place of the divine with the human, would survive the impending troubles. It was this new 'holy place' that would be preserved during the years of persecution and suffering.

The reference to '42 months' (11:2) is an important clue. This is exactly the 'three and a half times' of Daniel's prophecy, 42 months being three and a half years (Daniel 7:25; 12:7). This prophecy referred to the desecration of the temple by the Syrians under Antiochus in the second century BC. That temple was dramatically rebuilt and extended by Herod the Great in the first century BC.

Now, the prophecy of Daniel and the historical act of restoration become a picture of the life of the infant Church. She will suffer. It may seem, at times, that her enemies have triumphed, but God has promised that the 'gates of Hades [the grave] will not prevail against her' (Matthew 16:18). The Church, the new temple of God, built not of bricks and stone but of its living members, will survive. Once the time of persecution is over, it will emerge purified, strengthened and glorified. Already, as the visions have shown, those who perish in the tribulation share in the glory of the martyred saints around the throne.

Like all of the prophetic images in Revelation, these rather elusive ones about the temple and the Church have a relevant message for anxious Christians at any time, and in many ways their message is particularly important today. Since the conversion of the emperor Constantine in the fourth century, the Church in Europe has had a privileged position of power, both secular and religious. Consequently, Christians have become accustomed to exercising a powerful influence on government, laws, culture and social ethics. The Church's leaders—Popes, bishops, moderators and ordinary clergy— have been treated with great respect, their views published and broadcast, their teaching widely observed. Until com-paratively recent times, in many parts of what was called 'Christendom' the profession of Christian faith was essential for a person to progress in civic and social life, or even, in some cases, to be a legislator or judge. School days started with Christian worship. The Army, hospitals and prisons have had chaplains, monarchs have been crowned by archbishops, and presidents have been installed with Christian prayers and blessings.

In recent decades, however, the situation has begun to change. The secularisation of society in most Western countries has led to a gradual dilution of the influence of the Church. Sometimes this is attributed to the need to recognise that many of those societies are now multi-faith, with a large minority of citizens who are Muslim, Hindu, Sikh or Jewish, although most of those people do not want to live in an essentially secular society.

Those who have led the movement against Christian privileges generally do so for a number of other motives. Some argue it on grounds of justice. Many people in Western Europe, for instance, are demonstrably not religious, so why should they have religion 'thrust upon them'? Others attack Christian privilege (as they see it) because they regard all religious beliefs as irrational, throwbacks to an era of superstition and bigotry. Yet others do so because they see the diminishing numbers of practising Christians and resent propping up a collapsing and outdated mode of living.

Whatever the reasons, the results are the same. Instead of looking up to the Church, an increasing number of people, including many influential opinion-formers, look down on it. There's no doubt that many Christians feel under threat, their cherished beliefs ridiculed and rejected, their very place in society questioned.

In such a situation, how do Christians react? Some write indignant letters to the newspapers and the religious press, demanding greater respect for the Christian faith and its public practice, but most, it seems, reluctantly accept that the tide is strong against them and probably irreversible, at any rate in the short term. Some, perhaps many, are secretly anxious that the trend will never be reversed, and that the Christian Church across the world, the repository of the gospel itself, the jewel in heaven's crown, will eventually be swept away in a tidal wave of secularism.

The remedy for their anxiety is hidden in the vision recorded at the beginning of Revelation 11. The critics and secularists can only touch the 'outer courts' of the Church. They can pick away at the institution, at the outward trappings of religion, at its footholds in political and social life, but they can't touch the Holy Place, the spiritual heart of the Body of Christ. That is inviolable, because it is part of ultimate reality, the eternal truth of the Creator himself. The reality of religion is not the institution; indeed, it is nothing visible or tangible. It is the kingdom of God which, as Jesus said, can't be placed 'here' or 'there' because it is 'within you'—or, perhaps more precisely, 'among you' (Luke 17:21). That is the true Holy Place, the sanctuary of the divine presence among his human creatures.

In this same vision we are also introduced to the idea of the 'city' (11:8). Cities were as much a feature of the ancient world as they are of the modern one, although they were not as big, of course. Jericho was one of the earliest, but ancient history is full of their names: Babylon, Rome, Athens, Memphis, Alexandria, Antioch, Jerusalem. At different times each had its day of glory; in each case the glory faded as riches and power moved to another centre.

The cities remained, as places of commerce, of security, of government and power. Their walls and gates existed to protect the inhabitants and their possessions. Their watchmen stood on the towers to warn of danger or to announce the dawn of a new day. The rural people came in during daylight to do business, to buy and sell or to worship in the city's temples. The city represented human life at its most organised and human power in its greatest splendour.

The cities also enclosed much that was evil: the exploitation of the poor, the enslavement of alien captives brought inside its walls as plunder from foreign wars, the often arbitrary and cruel use of absolute power by its rulers. Chapter 11 takes us beyond the temple and its courts to the city itself, and this one is not a pleasant sight.

It is first described as 'Sodom and Egypt' (v. 8), though the identification is qualified by rather a strange adverb, translated in the NRSV as 'prophetically'. It could also mean 'allegorically', or 'spiritually'. In other words, this is not a geographical identification but a visionary one. Sodom was the place of corruption and sin; Egypt was the place of captivity and slavery. So this city is a place of evil: indeed, Jerusalem is also drawn into the picture, 'where also their Lord was crucified'. In other words, this city represents any human society that is defying God or deliberately opposing his will, or exploiting, enslaving or corrupting his children.

In this strange city—Sodom/Egypt/Jerusalem—stand two witnesses, described as 'two olive trees' and 'two lampstands' (vv. 3–4). They are 'two' because, as we've seen, 'two' is the symbol of testimony. The clue to understanding the identity of these witnesses is in the book of the prophet Zechariah, where a lampstand is positioned between two olive trees in a prophecy that identifies Zerubbabel as the true king and Joshua as the rightful high priest (Zechariah 3:1; 4:2–6). The lampstands represent the Holy Spirit and the olive trees the sacred oil that anointed the high priests, so it would seem that these witnesses represent the true Church, the 'royal priesthood' (1 Peter 2:9) and the community of the Holy Spirit.

So, even in days of evil, fear or corruption, the witnesses stand their ground. The Church of Christ is still there in Babylon/Rome, alive with the life of God and challenging people to turn from darkness and embrace the light of Christ.

It seemed, in the vision, that for a while the powers of evil had silenced this witness, just as the Church under persecution sometimes seems to disappear from view. However, after a while ('three and a half days', v. 9) the witnessing community was revived and, in response to its message and example, 'the rest of the people' (those who had survived an earthquake) 'gave glory to the God of heaven' (v. 13).

It's impossible to force a vision like this into precise details—impossible and futile. The central message of all these visions is the same, really. No matter what happens, no matter how powerful the opposition appears to be or how terrible the circumstances are, the true Church remains, God is still God, and his eternal purpose holds good. Indeed, as the heavenly voices now declare, 'The kingdom of the world has become the kingdom of our Lord and of his Messiah' (v. 15). The tense of the verb here is known as 'prophetic future': so certain is the prophecy that it's as if the events have already happened, although in fact they still lie in the future. The kingdom of this world has become the kingdom of our Lord in the purpose of God, so, to the eye of faith, it is already fulfilled. That is the explanation of the mystery; that is the answer to the ultimate questions.

In the rest of the book of Revelation, we shall see how contrasting aspects of the nature of a city are found in its visions. The city is a place of security and social value. It needs and can respond to the witness of the Church. Yet, at the same time, it is vulnerable to corruption, sin and the abuse of power. We shall find that all of these facets, and more, are vividly portrayed in its story, until the unfolding of the final magnificent vision of the eternal City of God.

Finding the safe place

Revelation 11–12

As the central message of these chapters unfolds, we can begin to see the working out of God's purpose. His adversaries, the dragon (Satan, supernatural evil) and the 'beast' (human evil), are revealed and confronted with the mystery of the birth of the child who will eventually be the means of their defeat.

And war broke out in heaven; Michael and his angels fought against the dragon. The dragon and his angels fought back, but they were defeated, and there was no longer any place for them in heaven. The great dragon was thrown down, that ancient serpent, who is called the Devil and Satan, the deceiver of the whole world—he was thrown down to the earth, and his angels were thrown down with him. Then I heard a loud voice in heaven, proclaiming, 'Now have come the salvation and the power and the kingdom of our God and the authority of his Messiah, for the accuser of our comrades has been thrown down, who accuses them day and night before our God. But they have conquered him by the blood of the Lamb and by the word of their testimony, for they did not cling to life even in the face of death.'

REVELATION 12:7–11

That vision of eternal security represented by the new Jerusalem, the city of God, must wait. First we have the consequences of the trumpet blast of the seventh angel (11:15—12:17). They are indisputably spectacular but, as usual, they are preceded by a glimpse into the heavenly throne room, to remind us that real power lies there and not in the hands of God's enemies, whether human or angelic. The nations may 'rage' (11:18) but the Lord God Almighty has 'taken [his] great power and begun to reign' (v. 17). We see the ark of the covenant, the sign of God's presence among his people, the vision accompanied by 'flashes of lightning, rumblings, peals of thunder, an earthquake, and heavy hail'(v. 19). What we are about to witness, then, are the death throes of the opposition, not the overthrow of the kingdom of God.

This means that although the events about to be revealed are terrifying, we should see the unfolding story as reassuring rather than worrying. Everything that will happen is within the boundaries of God's purpose. Nothing that will occur can take him by surprise or change the inevitable final victory of the Lamb upon the throne.

So the heavenly stage for the final battle opens before our eyes. A great 'portent' (12:1) appears in heaven: significantly, John calls it a *semeion* in Greek, the same word that the Gospel of John uses for the miracles of Jesus, usually translated as 'sign'. As in that Gospel, we should look for profound meaning here: there is more to it than meets the eye. A pregnant 'woman clothed with the sun, with the moon under her feet, and on her head a crown of twelve stars' is about to give birth. Then appears another sign, a 'great red dragon, with seven heads and ten horns, and seven diadems on his heads', standing before the woman in order to devour the child as soon as it is born (vv. 3–4).

Who is the woman, and what is the identity of the dragon? Thousands of words have been written in answer to those questions. Not surprisingly, medieval writers identified the woman with the Blessed Virgin Mary, thus giving rise to artistic representations of her crowned with twelve stars. However, although the woman is clearly intended to represent the mother of the Messiah, the later part of the vision raises problems about her identification with Mary in a literal sense. This is, after all, a 'sign' and the language is prophetic, not factual. There are clues here, too—echoes of a prophecy of Isaiah about 'mother Zion' (66:7–9), and references to her 'children' being persecuted, with the dragon 'making war' on them (Revelation 12:17).

The most convincing identification of the woman, for me, is with 'Zion', called by Paul 'the mother of us all' (Galatians 4:26, KJV)—that is, of all Christ's believing children. She is the embryonic Church, the mother of the whole messianic community. We are then free, if we wish, to see Mary the mother of Jesus in this sense as the 'mother' of that Church, which would consist of the sons and daughters of faith in her Son.

The dragon surely poses fewer problems, because eventually he is identified with Satan, the adversary of God. Faced with the birth of the Messiah, God's chosen Saviour and Deliverer, he is forced into desperate action, trying to snatch the child away and destroy him. The story being enacted in this vision is not of the birth of Jesus at Bethlehem but the 'battle' of Gethsemane and Golgotha, in which God's Messiah and God's Adversary fought the final and decisive conflict between light and darkness. The resurrection confirmed that victory lay with God and his anointed Son, who was 'declared to be Son of God with power according to the Spirit of holiness by resurrection from the dead' (Romans 1:4). So the woman's son is 'snatched away and taken to God and to his throne' (Revelation 12:5).

All of this probably seems unnecessarily opaque to us today. Why not tell it how it is? Why wrap up the story of our salvation in such complicated imagery? There seem to be two answers to those questions. The first is that at the time when John was recording these visions, he needed to shroud them in visionary language so that they could be circulated around the churches without being too specific about the identity of the characters involved. This is especially true when we come, very shortly, to the identity of the 'beast' who persecutes the Church.

The second reason—and the one that makes these visions meaningful to us—is that only such visionary language can truly do justice to concepts that cannot be reduced to ordinary patterns of speech. How on earth can notions of heaven itself, or of the cosmic struggle between Light and Darkness, be portrayed except in some kind of metaphorical or allegorical language? These visions are powerful aids to understanding—not to simplify the concepts, because they aren't simple, but to make what is literally incomprehensible (because it deals with a reality beyond our understanding) accessible to the sons and daughters of earth. With imagination and faith we can read the words, see the visions and share the revelation.

That vision, of the woman, the child and the dragon, portrays in imaginative language the triumph of Jesus through his death and resurrection. Like a parenthesis in the account and, in logical terms, parallel to it, we have the even more bizarre vision of 'war in heaven' (12:7–9). The stage is occupied by two angelic armies, that of the archangel Michael on the one hand, and of 'the dragon and his angels' on the other.

We must understand that this is not war around the heavenly throne or anything like that, but a battle fought out on the invisible but real battlefield of the spiritual dimension of reality, a dimension that is normally, and mercifully, hidden from human view. This, of course, is the very dimension that these visions are concerned with. The war is violent ('the dragon and his angels fought back'), but eventually Michael and his hosts prevail, and the dragon, now clearly identified as 'that ancient serpent, who is called the Devil and Satan, the deceiver of the whole world' (v. 9), is thrown down to earth, and his army with him. For now, that will be their secondary battlefield, but (as Revelation later makes clear) only for a limited time.

Is this strange story of 'war in heaven' of any relevance to a reader today, especially one seeking answers to questions about the presence of evil and suffering in a world created by a good and loving God? The answer must be 'yes', because what it tells us, placed as it is alongside the lonely 'battle' of Gethsemane and Calvary, is that our forgiveness and redemption were not lightly won. Perhaps we shy away from facing it, but the truth hammered home here is that Jesus fought a very real battle against very real opposition. That agonised prayer in Gethsemane ('Father, if it is possible, let this cup pass from me': Matthew 26:39) was wrung from the lips of the Son of God by his vivid realisation of the reality of the power of evil that he was to confront on the cross.

The cross was no token conflict or premeditated walkover. Jesus died a real death for real sin. The 'lamb of God' bore away the sin of the world (John 1:29) but it was no easy burden. The picture of a cosmic battle waged between good and evil may seem primitive and even superstitious to us, but it is a portrayal—or 'sign'—of a profound truth about the world in which we live. We don't have to think in terms of winged warriors in glowing robes or horned demons in red; the voices and faces of evil, oppression, exploitation, cruelty and injustice are all around us. They are in God's world not because he put them there but because human sin, the misuse of the divine gift of moral choice by creatures who thought they knew better than their Creator, has itself created them. They are the visible evidences of 'Satan' (the Hebrew word means 'adversary' or 'opponent'). They are the darkness that opposes the light. Human or spiritual, they are, we might say, His Heavenly Majesty's Disloyal Opposition.

These pictures of the final conflict between Light and Darkness tell us that in the end, in the ultimate purpose of God, the creation will be purged of everything that is evil. Just as the woman's child was triumphantly raised to heaven after his victory over sin and death on the cross, so the same victory of God over evil will be seen over the whole of his creation. The devil and his angels (think of them in whatever way you wish) will be defeated and eventually banished from the earth as well as from that heavenly stage.

Some may feel that that is cold comfort for people caught up in the trials and tribulations of everyday life here and now, that the message amounts to no more than 'Cheer up! In the end God will put it all right, but not until you're dead!' However, there's no doubt that John, in recording these visions, was seeking to offer genuine encouragement and hope to his readers there and then, not simply at an unspecified time in the future. Yes, heaven lay ahead for them if they remained faithful, but now, while the trials and tribulations were going on, when days of persecution came or individuals suffered personal tragedy and loss, they were not to fear. That was, after all, the opening message of the book from the mouth of the risen Jesus (1:17), and nothing has changed its truth.

What is this encouragement and hope? It lies hidden or, rather, waiting to be recognised in the story enacted in these two visions—of the Messiah-child who died and rose, and of the victory of Michael and his angels over the rebellious spirits on the cosmic stage. The encouragement and hope, in other words, is that victory is now. The dragon of opposition, dismay or fear may roar but he cannot touch the Lord's anointed. The forces of evil may seem to take control but in truth they are ultimately powerless.

We could put it this way: would you rather be on the dragon's side or the Messiah-child's? Would you choose to identify with the rebellious spirits or with Michael and the hosts of heaven? With which party does hope and encouragement lie?

On the one side stand the visions of evil—ugly, monstrous, menacing but ultimately pointless and self-destructive. On the other side are contrasting visions of goodness—the rainbow, the angels, the saints around the throne, the songs and the sweet incense, 'the beauty of holiness' (as Monsell's hymn puts it). The truth is that sooner or later we have to make the choice between them, because, as we have seen, there is a spiritual conflict between good and evil, darkness and light, and there are no neutrals in this war. But—and here is the message of these visions—the safe place, the secure centre, is with the One who sits on the throne and with the Lamb. Those who are his have no reason, now or in the future, to be afraid.

The two beasts

Revelation 13–14

The two beasts who appear in these chapters seem to represent secular power, which, wittingly or unwittingly, is helping to fulfil the objectives of 'Satan', the adversary of good and the personification of evil. They are not ostensibly ugly—one wears diadems and the other has some of the appearance of a lamb—but they are using their worldly power to enslave the nations, oppose the people of God and claim divine authority over the whole world.

And I saw a beast rising out of the sea, having ten horns and seven heads; and on its horns were ten diadems, and on its heads were blasphemous names... Also it causes all, both small and great, both rich and poor, both free and slave, to be marked on the right hand or the forehead, so that no one can buy or sell who does not have the mark, that is, the name of the beast or the number of its name. This calls for wisdom: let anyone with understanding calculate the number of the beast, for it is the number of a person. Its number is six hundred and sixty-six.

REVELATION 13:1, 16–18

The visions in this central part of Revelation have covered many of the causes of human anxiety and fear: war and violence, plague and famine, earthquake and storm. They have also evoked images of our more hidden fears about what might happen in the future, or about unseen, malign evil invading the normality of daily life. In between the horrors, we have paid many visits to the heavenly throne room, as though to reassure us that there is a steady hand in control of the universe. However bad things may seem, creation has not descended into anarchy.

Now we meet the 'beast rising out of the sea'. It has ten horns on seven heads; on its horns are ten diadems and on its head 'blasphemous names'. This beast is an accessory of the dragon, which presumably means that he is doing the work of Satan. He is then joined by another beast, this time rising out of the earth (v. 11). This one is less horrifying. Indeed, he bears the horns of a 'lamb', the picture of innocence. However, he is fully empowered to do the work of the dragon (Satan) and the other beast, though perhaps in a more subtle way.

This beast requires ordinary people, rich and poor, to worship him, and marks those who do so on their right hands or foreheads, in imitation of the mark of the cross given to the followers of Jesus at baptism. Unless people bear this mark, they cannot buy or sell: they are, in effect, outcasts from society.

Eventually we are given a clue as to the identity of this beast. He has an identifying number (in the numeric system explained earlier) and it is 666. As we have already seen, that is the name 'Nero Caesar' in numeric code form. The beast, then, is the Empire and the Emperor—the imperial power that would, for a time, try to wipe the Church off the face of the earth. We may therefore assume that the two beasts, one from the sea and one from the earth, are worldly power, perhaps expressed in the naval power that dominates the sea and military power that holds the land.

It is interesting to see the precise nature of the persecution that the second beast perpetrates on the followers of Christ. It is true that those who refused to 'worship the image of the beast' (v. 15)—perhaps, to burn incense at an altar before the imperial image—could be killed by the sword, but most weren't. The general pressure was less crude than that: Nero knew that he couldn't expect to exterminate the entire Christian population, which by then probably ran to scores of thousands of people, at least. So only those who worshipped the emperor, who bore the mark of the beast on their right hand or forehead (v. 16), were free to buy or sell in the market.

The Christians would be not physically persecuted but economically and socially excluded, a more subtle form of psychological pressure, the pressure to conform in order to be allowed to participate in society. Why jib at the most nominal gesture of approval when refusal has such unpleasant consequences? Why is a tiny pinch of incense too much to ask of a loyal Christian citizen?

As the vision moves on, we see the outcome of all this. There are those who bear the beast's mark on their foreheads, followers (however unwittingly) of a power that devolves from the dragon himself (12:18; 13:11), and there are those who have the name of the Lamb 'written on their foreheads'

(14:1). Their number is given as 144,000, which is simply saying that it is utterly comprehensive, that it includes all who come to him, the number being (as we saw earlier) the multiplication of completeness (twelve times twelve times a thousand). The company of heaven is not exclusive but inclusive: 'let anyone who wishes take the water of life as a gift' (22:17). Nevertheless, they belong to the Lamb; they bear his mark; they are, like it or not, distinct and different from the followers of the beast, who bear *his* mark.

Throughout the ages, this has been a constant challenge to faith—the price of being 'different'; literally, nonconformity. It asks the believer to stand out from the crowd, to swim against the tide, to be identified as the odd one out, the awkward person who makes a terrible fuss about as small a thing as a pinch of incense on the altar.

It's not hard to think of parallels in contemporary society: the nurse who has a conscientious objection to abortion on demand, the school teacher required to instruct pre-teens in the techniques of contraception, the Christian pacifist abused for his or her opposition to involvement in armed conflict. There is always a price to pay, but, for members of what may sometimes feel like a beleaguered minority, it is often hard to know where lines should be drawn, and when conscience becomes sheer cussedness or something dangerously like fanaticism. The call of this vision in Revelation is to 'endurance and faith' (v. 10), and the test is surely whether the actions required of us would deny that faith or undermine that endurance.

Over the centuries Christians have had to face this challenge, as they do today. They have faced it in China, particularly at the time of the Cultural Revolution in the mid-20th century. They faced it under the Soviet regime and in Communist Eastern Europe. More recently, Christians in some Muslim lands have found these pressures so intense that they have felt the need to leave home and country. Sadly, sometimes they have faced it from their fellow Christians: the very word 'non-conformist' has its roots in the religious pressure applied to groups of believers in past centuries. To live peacefully with the society in which we find ourselves, as faithful citizens and good neighbours, is a Christian duty, but sometimes the pressure to conform to that which we know to be contrary to the gospel as we understand it requires a person to stand apart—yes, to 'be different'.

There are two different fears at work here, each of which can trouble us at different times or in different circumstances. The first and most obvious, as we have seen, is the pressure to conform. For anyone with a conscience, this can at times be very painful. Our world is very skilful in the art of conformity, so that if we feel unable or unwilling to go with the flow of contemporary moral or social judgments, we feel not just odd but excluded. We can see this in many areas of life—family values, sexual morality, personal honesty and less easily defined areas like the use of crude language or cruel and abusive humour. We may have no wish to appear prudish or judgmental, but simply taking a stand on some of these issues may mean that we are seen as 'outsiders' in the present social consensus.

The other fear is of compromise. We are aware of how easily we can be sucked into accepting what, at heart, we know to be unacceptable. The 'tiny pinch of incense' for us may be to slip into casual blasphemy. Just think how widespread is the use of the exclamation 'Oh my God!' in everyday language. It may be to slip into a lifestyle that contradicts what we know to be Christlike. It may be a subtle dilution of our personal standards of honesty or faithfulness in the workplace or the home. We have all known these pressures, and such is the effect of them that, at times, we may not even realise how far we have shifted. The 'pinch of incense' is not, in itself, the issue: it never was. The issue is allegiance. Christians may, and do, differ over specific issues of behaviour, lifestyle and ethics, but they are required to be united in their allegiance to Christ, whose sign we bear.

It may be that, in different circumstances or cultural settings, Christians will reach different conclusions about a range of issues. A relatively trivial example would be women covering their heads during worship (see 1 Corinthians 11:6); more serious issues might include birth control, gay relationships, assisted suicide, pacifism and stem cell research. It is manifestly true that people owing an unswerving allegiance to Christ may take different stances on such issues, but that does not call their allegiance to Christ into question. To bear his sign is a fearful responsibility and a wonderful privilege, but it doesn't automatically confer unanimity of understanding over every ethical or theological question.

The apostle Paul told the Christians at Colosse to 'do everything in the name of the Lord Jesus' (Colossians 3:17). That seems a very good basic test. This issue that lies before me, this decision over whether or not to do something or refrain from doing something: can I do it, or refrain from doing it, 'in the name of the Lord Jesus'? Would doing it compromise my allegiance to him? Would refraining from doing it enhance that allegiance (or simply make me feel pious)? The Christians in ancient Rome did not feel that they could burn incense at the Emperor's altar 'in the name of the Lord Jesus', and surely they were right. However, Paul didn't make the issue of eating meat 'offered to idols' into a question of allegiance to Christ (1 Corinthians 8) so much as of sensitivity to other people's feelings.

The beast marks his adherents, rather like a farmer branding his sheep. They are his, and they do his bidding. But—and this is the issue here—so does Jesus. As we have seen, his followers also bear a mark. The sign of the cross marked on the forehead with oil at baptism (an ancient rite still practised in most Christian churches) may wash away in an hour or two, but, spiritually speaking, its mark is indelible. 'Christ claims you for his own,' the Anglican service reminds us. 'Receive the sign of the cross.' We are his and, because we are his, we do his bidding, we are members of his flock, and we are in the hands of the good Shepherd. We 'follow the Lamb wherever he goes' (14:4).

From these first 14 chapters of Revelation, with their sometimes horrific, sometimes glorious visions, we have been shown a world with which, in slightly less colourful terms, we are generally familiar. It is a world of light and darkness, joy and suffering, fear and hope. On the cosmic stage are figures of ugliness and evil: the dragon, the beasts, the locusts and strange horses and their riders. They truthfully portray a world that is sometimes frightening and menacing, a world where many suffer.

We should note yet again that the visions portray a world

with a calm centre. Time and again, and whenever the visions seem to be at their most terrifying, we are given another glimpse of the heavenly throne room. There we see the One who sits on the throne, the Creator God; beside him we see the Lamb bearing the marks of slaughter, the Son of God who 'takes away the sin of the world' (John 1:29); we see the ever-active Spirit of God, symbolised by the lampstands with their constantly burning lights. Here, too, are the angelic emissaries, carrying out the orders from the throne. It is a picture of serene order and control.

Yet the world, as we know both from our present experience and from the truth of these visions in Revelation, has many frightening elements. We have seen the confirmation of our everyday experience of life, that it is scarily unpredictable. At the same time, we are constantly aware of the presence of sin. There is rampant injustice. The unavoidable risks of life are multiplied by greed and the presence of violence and exploitation. We do not 'make' earthquakes and floods, but their impact always seems to be most devastating for the poor and vulnerable.

'Do not be afraid' remains, however, the underlying message of Revelation, and it is time that we looked at what this means in practice. What answers does it offer to our anxieties, granted (as its visions freely concede) that there seems to be so much in our daily experience of which to be afraid? Let's turn, then, to look at the answers it offers—first, the wrong answer, and finally the genuine divine answer.

Babylon: money, power and might

Revelation 15–18

These chapters begin, as so often, with a vision of heaven, where they are singing the 'song of Moses... and the song of the Lamb', the celebration of liberty and redemption. We then quickly move on to terrible scenes of disaster and judgment, including the battle of Armageddon and the utter destruction of Babylon in all its splendour. It is a cruel picture but it is, in visionary terms, the inevitable judgment of those who put their trust in human power, riches and indulgence.

After this I saw another angel coming down from heaven, having great authority; and the earth was made bright with his splendour. He called out with a mighty voice, 'Fallen, fallen is Babylon the great!' ... And the merchants of the earth weep and mourn for her, since no one buys their cargo any more, cargo of gold, silver, jewels and pearls, fine linen, purple, silk and scarlet, all kinds of scented wood, all articles of ivory, all articles of costly wood, bronze, iron, and marble, cinnamon, spice, incense, myrrh, frankincense, wine, olive oil, choice flour and wheat, cattle and sheep, horses and chariots, slaves—and human lives.

'The fruit for which your soul longed has gone from you, and all your dainties and your splendour are lost to you, never to be found again!' … 'Alas, alas, the great city, clothed in fine linen, in purple and scarlet, adorned with gold, with jewels, and with pearls! For in one hour all this wealth has been laid waste!' … 'And the sound of harpists and minstrels and of flautists and trumpeters will be heard in you no more; and an artisan of any trade will be found in you no more; and the sound of the millstone will be heard in you no more… for your merchants were the magnates of the earth, and all nations were deceived by your sorcery.'

REVELATION 18:1–2, 11–14, 16–17, 22, 23B

These chapters begin with a typical apocalyptic contrast. Seven angels stand before God, holding seven golden bowls containing seven plagues. At the same time, we hear a song of triumph sounding from the lips of those who have 'conquered the beast'. It is described as 'the song of Moses… and the song of the Lamb' (15:1–4). The mention of seven plagues and of Moses and the Lamb inevitably conjures up echoes of the events surrounding the first Passover—the plagues wreaked on Pharaoh and his people, the lamb that each Hebrew family was required to kill and eat, and then the triumphant crossing of the Red Sea and the start of the long trek to freedom and the promised land (see Exodus 10—14).

The singers of the song are those who have 'conquered' the beast, even though he is not yet conquered. The verb in verse 2 is, in fact, in the present tense: 'those who conquer'. By their faith and commitment, they are conquering the beast now, and will soon see the fulfilment of that conquest. This maintains the general stance of Revelation about the present and the future: its message of hope is both 'now' and 'then'. The people can sing the song of Moses and the Lamb because, in the perspective of heaven, their freedom is already won.

This also explains why the presence of the angels with the bowls of plagues alongside celebrations of holy victory is not incongruous. Their bowls are instruments both of judgment and redemption, because they will defeat evil and set the faithful free. The plagues of Egypt, in Moses' day, were a judgment on the cruelty of Pharaoh and his servants but they were also the means by which the Hebrew people were freed from slavery and set on the road to the land of promise. As the angels in Revelation release their plagues one by one on the earth (several of them mirroring the plagues of Egypt), the phrase recurs: 'they did not repent of their deeds' (see 16:9, 11). Like Pharaoh, the people hardened their hearts rather than repent (see, for example, Exodus 8:32; 9:7).

Before the last plague is released, the demonic forces assemble for the final battle with 'God the Almighty' at a place called Harmagedon (16:14–16). It's often spelt 'Armageddon' and is used nowadays to describe any decisive and cataclysmic confrontation. Harmagedon means 'the hill of Megiddo', Megiddo being a town in the centre of Israel which had been the site of several historic battles (see, for instance, Judges 5:19; 2 Kings 23:29; 2 Chronicles 35:22). Megiddo, however, was in the centre of a plain, as these Old Testament references make clear, and quite a distance from the nearest hill, suggesting that the language here is visionary and metaphorical rather than literal. The enemies of God had often gathered on what the Bible calls 'high places'—sites for idolatrous worship. The first mention of them is in Leviticus 26:30, but 58 more times the Israelites are warned of their corrupting presence. Now, as the final conflict between good and evil is to take place, the enemies of God gather in a 'high place', the hill of Megiddo.

The last, seventh plague involves a spectacular earthquake 'such as had not occurred since people were on the earth' (16:18), with its epicentre at 'the great city', Babylon (v. 19). The moment of judgment on the imperial power of Rome has come at last.

We can imagine the seer John, deep in his trance-like state on the island of Patmos, at some time in the late first century. He is a Christian in an empire that has, for the present, set its face against the young Church, which it sees, probably rightly, as being deeply opposed to its own values and aspirations.

At the centre of that empire stands the great city of Rome and its all-powerful Emperor. Its armies control the whole of the world that John knows. Its prefects, legates and pro-curators rule the provinces. Its merchants control the world's commerce. Great arenas have been built for the games and spectacles that constitute its principle leisure pursuits, often cruel and bloody. Its religion, a strange mixture of incred-ible stories of mythological gods and goddesses along with worship of the State and especially its emperor, is celebrated in thousands of shrines and temples. The patricians and the wealthy merchant classes of Rome are able to live in un-ashamed and wanton indulgence. Drunkenness and sexual exploitation are commonplace, and there is a prevailing atmosphere of crudity in much upper-class society.

Of course, it would be wrong to give the impression that every aspect of Roman rule was bad. In practical terms, the empire ruled well. Aqueducts and roads transformed the life of farflung communities. Roman law, while harsh by today's standards, was fundamentally fair. Its legions, well trained and well disciplined, maintained the *Pax Romana* ('Roman peace') over most of Europe, north Africa and the Near East. The Greco-Roman world had also produced one of the most impressive cultures of human history, with its philosophers, playwrights and poets still honoured, read and performed two millennia later. In the first century of the Christian era, that culture had moved beyond its golden age but the glorious legacy remained.

Certainly, before the days of the active persecution of the Church by the State, the apostles insisted that Christians should be loyal and obedient citizens of the empire, honouring the emperor, paying taxes and obeying its laws so far as conscience allowed (see, for instance, Romans 13:1–7; Titus 3:1; 1 Peter 2:13–17). However, things had changed by the time Revelation was written. Where the Church was concerned, persecution, actual and threatened, had become a fact. For the Christians, who believed that the Lord God was king of all the earth, Rome must have seemed the ultimate contradiction of that belief, and the divine worship demanded for her emperor was the final blasphemy. The great empire, far from being (as some had hoped) the ultimate answer to human fears and anxieties, had simply created new and terrible ones.

So it must have been with great anticipation that John watched his visions moving inexorably to a moment of divine judgment. Plague, war, famine, flood and earthquake were indeed terrible but nothing was as terrible, as infinitely threatening, as the massive power of the empire of Rome. If, as seemed likely from the recent persecutions, Rome had indeed set its face against God and his Christ, then the final battle had surely been signalled. If God was God, and sat on the throne of the universe, how could a mortal like the emperor of Rome, however powerful, stand against him? How long would the Lord tolerate this monstrous blasphemy to hold sway over so much of the earth?

Now, it seemed, as John observed the visions, the moment of divine retribution had come at last. The avenging angel held the sickle of judgment; the days of the blasphemous city were numbered. It is never called by its actual name in these visions. It becomes 'Babylon', the great city of past ages that was, for centuries, the foremost enemy of God's people. The fact that 'Babylon' is indeed Rome, however, is beyond doubt. Everything revealed about it could only possibly apply to the empire that had its centre on the seven hills by the River Tiber.

If we are ever tempted to think that the answer to the world's anxieties and fears lies in worldly power, military might or economic muscle, these visions of the judgment of Babylon should make us think again. It's interesting to see which aspects of the life of the Roman empire are highlighted for special judgment. In some respects, many of them seem morally neutral, yet from God's perspective they are deemed unacceptable.

For instance, in chapters 17 and 18 different aspects of the life of Rome/Babylon, now seen as a blasphemous woman, the 'mother of whores' (17:5), are picked out for special condemnation. She is several times accused of 'fornication', and others of committing 'fornication' with her (17:2, 4; 18:3, 9). In English, to fornicate is to have sexual relations with someone to whom one is not married. While there's no doubt that such activities went on in the city, the word seems to have a wider meaning here. 'Fornicate' comes from a Latin root based on the slang word for brothel, so perhaps the implication is of the buying and selling of people's minds and bodies, or the misusing of people and relationships for sordid ends. The actual Greek word used here certainly carries implications of general uncleanness, lewdness and even incest, but its connection to 'merchants' (18:3) perhaps also suggests the 'prostitution' of principle and honest dealing in the interest of profit.

Luxury is also targeted. The merchants have grown rich through trading in cargoes of luxurious items—gold, silver, pearls, fine linen and silks, spices and perfumes. Tacked on the end of the list are three grim words: 'and human lives' (v. 13). This prosperity came at a price: the death of slaves, perhaps, sweating below decks in the crowded galleys where they plied the oars of great cargo vessels, or women and boys bought and sold for sex.

Fashion and entertainment are denounced, too—the musicians and entertainers, and the 'dainties and... splendour' (v. 14), the purple, scarlet and gold that adorned the rich. Honest labour—the millstone and the artisan—are no more. The wealth of 'Babylon' is not won by hard work or skilled hands, but by unscrupulous trading, the buying and selling of luxuries and the indulging of the powerful. The whole picture has an air of decadence about it. 'Babylon' is all show and little substance.

This is the great city-state, the epitome of humanity organised as though God did not exist. It is not difficult to relate the picture to much of life in today's world, where conspicuous affluence stands in cruel contrast to the poverty endured by much of the rest of humankind. It is this empty husk of pretension and glamour that dares to set itself up against God and his people, to terrify and dominate our hearts and minds. 'Babylon' is power, wealth, reputation, status—all the things that our fallen nature most craves, yet exposed here as fundamentally worthless.

Many of our fears are about our lack of power, wealth or status, or our feelings when confronted by others who have gained these assets. The fantasy of many an ordinary person is to win the lottery and join the ranks of the self-indulgent wielders of social and economic power. But to do so, says this vision, is to chase after a mere chimera, an impossible illusion. If we achieved it, we would find that it turned to dust in our hands.

'Babylon' does not offer the answer to our longings, anxieties and fears; power and wealth are not solutions to the human dilemma but, too often, are causes of it. The problems we face, the fears that haunt us, the anxieties we have about the present and the future, will not be solved by the application of selfish wealth and naked power. 'Babylon the Great' is fallen (18:2) and, so far as heaven is concerned, that is cause for angelic rejoicing.

Of course, 'Babylon' means more than just Rome, other-wise the end of Rome and her empire would have meant the end of the corrupting effects of greed and power on the human race. In fact, they have been ever present, from the earliest stories of biblical history to these visions of the end of time.

Perhaps the first biblical picture of 'Babylon' (in this metaphorical sense) is Babel. This rather strange story is recorded in Genesis 11—strange and yet, in a way, instantly recognisable as an illustration of a besetting human delusion. It is both a story and a parable.

As the descendants of Noah (now presumably a large tribe) migrated across the Middle East, they came to a plain in a land named as Shinar. Here they developed the manufacture of bricks and began to get ambitious ideas about building. The chronicler puts some marvellously revealing words into their mouths: 'Come, let us build ourselves a city, and a tower with its top in the heavens, and let us make a name for ourselves; otherwise we shall be scattered abroad upon the face of the whole earth' (v. 4).

The Lord Almighty 'came down' to see what they were up to, and was not impressed.

'Look,' he said, 'they are one people, and they have all one language; and this is only the beginning of what they will do; nothing that they propose to do will now be impossible for them. Come, let us go down, and confuse their language there, so that they will not understand one another's speech.' So the Lord scattered them abroad from there over the face of all the earth, and they left off building the city. Therefore it was called Babel, because there the Lord confused the language of all the earth; and from there the Lord scattered them abroad over the face of all the earth. (vv. 6–9)

While this story can hardly be taken as a scientific explanation of the way languages developed, as a parable it puts its finger on an important truth about human behaviour. These early property developers were trying to 'make a name' for themselves, setting up a centre of power, prestige and domination, even if it meant defying the will of God. It was the kind of arrogance that has marked so much of our history, right down to the worldwide banking crisis of 2008. 'Look, let's build a reputation; let's go for status; let's make our mark!' There speaks the genuine voice of Babel. The name means 'confused', and confusion, of course, was the outcome of their proud enterprise—as it so often is. Enterprise is not a bad thing: manifestly, the human race would never have left its caves and tents unless our enterprising ancestors had taken risks and made dreams come true. But the fuel for enterprise must not be status, power or greed, and that is where the Babel approach inevitably tends to lead. It is certainly the chief accusation laid by God against 'Babylon' in the book of Revelation.

History has seen many Babels, Babylons and Romes— great cities and great empires that have come and gone. They have achieved much, for which humanity should be grateful. Under wise leadership they have often created and shared wealth, improved the lot of ordinary people and led to advances in science, philosophy and the arts. Too often, though, the leadership has itself been corrupted by the heady delusions of power. Wealth has not been shared but indulged. The rich merchants and the kings have prospered while the masses toiled, rowed, sowed and planted and received a meagre share of the good things created by the city-state. To Babel, Babylon and Rome we could add Israel under Solomon (1 Kings 11). We could also, with some justification, add the British Empire of recent memory, and present-day financial centres like Wall Street and the City of London. Just as Babylon and Rome did many good things but fell in the end under the sheer weight of naked ambition and hubris, there is the constant danger that the institutions revered by our society, and by which we live, might fall for the same delusions of power.

As we have seen, the visions of Revelation pull no punches. The great sin of Babylon/Rome was not that it was powerful but that it misused power. It is not that cities are uniquely sinful but that, as centres of enterprise, wealth and power, they exemplify both the capacity of the human spirit to achieve great things and the tendency of human sinfulness eventually to misuse its gifts. The city stands for all that is worthy and good about humanity and, at the same time, all that is most weak and corrupt. Alongside the institutions of power—the palaces, the banks, the stock markets—we can find the mean homes of the powerless, the poor and the enslaved. Like the would-be builders of Babel, the city's towers reach to the sky but in their shadow live those who find it hard even to look up.

The ancient cities had walls and their gates were locked at night to keep out enemies, criminals and strangers. Today, our cities have no physical gates, although there are mental ones. Some people, for instance, find living in cities difficult, even frightening, with the crowds, the noise, and the frequent presence of crime and violence. Others love living in an urban context, finding the buzz of activity exciting and the noise and close presence of neighbours reassuring. Cities often have what amount to ghettoes, however, where only people of certain ethnic groups or religions are welcome, or where everyone is poor or, conversely, everyone is rich.

The truth is that our cities embody the whole of life: there are luxury and greed but there are also poverty and need. There are criminality and sin but there is also the brave witness of the Church and its members. There are fear and anxiety because, in the city, life is constantly changing and uncertain, but there are also faith and love and companionship, because true humanity also expresses itself in these ways.

From the perspective of the visions in Revelation, however, there is little doubt that the earthly city is seen as society organised as though God didn't exist, or, if he does, as though his moral and ethical principles can simply be ignored. That is Babylon; that is Rome. God's people may need to live in such cities but they cannot allow themselves to become part of their way of thinking: they are surely called to be salt to bring purity to the city's joys, and light to illuminate its darkest corners.

Conflict: the heart of the gospel

Revelation 19—20

Once again, scenes of judgment are preceded by a vision of heaven, songs of worship and the promise that 'the Lord our God the Almighty reigns'. We move on to what proves to be the final judgments—the unlocking of the 'pit', the capture of the 'beast' and the 'false prophet' and then their despatch, along with other dark elements, into the 'lake of fire'. The cleansing of the creation is now complete!

Then I saw heaven opened, and there was a white horse! Its rider is called Faithful and True, and in righteousness he judges and makes war. His eyes are like a flame of fire, and on his head are many diadems; and he has a name inscribed that no one knows but himself. He is clothed in a robe dipped in blood, and his name is called The Word of God. And the armies of heaven, wearing fine linen, white and pure, were following him on white horses. From his mouth comes a sharp sword with which to strike down the nations, and he will rule them with a rod of iron; he will tread the wine press of the fury of the wrath of God the

*Almighty. On his robe and on his thigh he has a name inscribed,
'King of kings and Lord of lords'.*

REVELATION 19:11–16

Most people won't need convincing that struggle and conflict
between good and evil are constant features of human life.
This is true both at a personal level and in the wider affairs of
communities and nations.

At the personal level, we can all echo the cry of the apostle
Paul: 'So I find it to be a law that when I want to do what is
good, evil lies close at hand. For I delight in the law of God in
my inmost self, but I see in my members another law at war
with the law of my mind, making me captive to the law of sin
that dwells in my members' (Romans 7:21–23). We are aware,
as he was, of the inner conflict, the battle of the conscience
against other inclinations, a battle that we sometimes win and
often lose. Even the most dedicated believer will experience
this inner conflict. Indeed, such a person will probably be
more aware of its reality than someone whose conscience has
been dulled by incessant surrender to the inclinations of self.

While life lasts, the struggle goes on. As the Scottish
preacher Alexander Whyte said, 'It's a sore fight to the end!'
The writer of the biblical letter to Hebrew Christians spoke
of their 'struggle against sin', in which they must not 'grow
weary or lose heart'. After all, he added, in that struggle they
have 'not yet resisted to the point of shedding… blood'
(Hebrews 12:3–4). The clear implication is that they might
one day.

The inner battle between what we know to be right and
what we recognise to be wrong is one of the things that de-

fine us as human beings. It is vividly portrayed in the Genesis story of the temptation of the first woman and the first man, the couple we know as Adam and Eve. We are morally autonomous, which simply means that we have the awesome responsibility of choice. We can follow conscience and the law of God or we can follow our own, often selfish preferences. While this requirement to choose, to engage in a struggle between right and wrong, is a constant burden, it is also a unique privilege.

The conflict at the individual level is also evident on the grand scale. I remember, as a sixth-former, studying European history and coming to the slightly depressing conclusion that it was mostly the chronicle of wars. Through the centuries, people have fought, sometimes with astonishing bravery, for all kinds of causes—some of them blatantly sinful (conquest, economic riches, vicious revenge) and sometimes for nobler ends (to resist slavery or oppose such evil ideologies as fascism).

Conflict and struggle are also the inspiration for much of our most admired literature. Think of Shakespeare's *Othello*, *The Merchant of Venice* or *Measure for Measure*—stories of agonised conflicts of conscience between right and wrong, mercy and greed, principle and self-indulgence.

It's not surprising, then, that the language of conflict is also prevalent in religious attitudes. The Christian life, for instance, has often been presented in terms of warfare in hymns such as 'Onward, Christian soldiers, marching as to war'. Indeed, the letter to the believers in Ephesus urges them to arm themselves with the equipment of a soldier on active service—although, significantly, the only offensive item recommended is 'the sword of the Spirit, which is the word of God' (see Ephesians 6:10–17).

Conflict and struggle are central to the biblical revelation. After all, Christianity is founded on the words and actions of a man who accepted, with tears, that he was engaged in a mortal struggle with evil and who died a violent death to defeat it. We cannot remove the cross from the creed. It stands reproduced on altars and in cemeteries, hanging around the necks of believers and crowning some of our noblest buildings, as a constant reminder that the Christian faith is about conflict. Our own observation of life, our greatest literature and art, simply confirm the biblical revelation.

It's interesting that as the book of Revelation moves to its climax, it is this element of conflict and struggle that predominates. Of course it has been present throughout the visions, but the battle between light and darkness, goodness and evil, God and his adversaries assumes an awesome intensity as we move through chapters 16—20. Indeed, we are in Hammer Horror territory: 'foul and painful sores', grotesque spirits like frogs, enormous hailstones 'each weighing about a hundred pounds' (see 16:2–21), a 'scarlet beast… full of blasphemous names' (17:3) and flesh-eating birds (19:17–18). The imagery is ugly, the language explicit, and the atmosphere, it has to be said, vengeful.

The motivating force behind this final struggle with the corrupting effect of evil appears to be what John calls 'the wrath of God' and even 'the wrath of the Lamb'. Throughout the visions of this book we have heard mention of this wrath, but in these chapters it is emphasised many times (see, for example, 16:1, 19; 19:15).

Once again, reading these passages today, we may feel shock. Isn't it true that 'God is love' (1 John 4:8)? How can a loving God feel wrath towards any of his creatures, however badly they have behaved? We struggle with the idea that God is about to wreak vengeance on those who have opposed his love and justice. Is he no longer the God of infinite mercy and forgiveness? Our cultural conditioning shapes our attitudes, and most of us, whether religious believers or not, prefer to look for the good in people and situations rather than what is indisputably evil and corrupt. Even if we can't, we certainly expect God to take a more liberal and forgiving approach to the weaknesses and moral failures of his creatures than we do.

We find the idea of wrath a strange one to apply to the God constantly addressed in the Bible as 'full of steadfast love' (see, for example, Psalm 33:5). Yet here in Revelation it is not only applied to the Lord God Almighty on his throne, but also to the Lamb-Redeemer who sits beside him. For us, 'wrath' means anger, temper, uncontrolled fury. Is that really what it means?

As usual, the question of translation comes in here. Two Greek words are used for 'wrath' in Revelation. One carries a sense of 'indignation', the other of a strong passion or mental emotion—something like 'outrage'. On one occasion (in the passage that heads this chapter), they are linked together—literally, 'the wine of the outrage of the indignation of God'. Whatever this 'wrath' is, it is not temper or uncontrolled fury.

Probably more helpful than wrestling with the subtleties of translation is to consider the example of Jesus. All four Gospels (rather unusually) record his outburst of anger in the temple, though John uniquely places it at the start rather than near the end of his ministry. The event was therefore deemed by all four writers to be both memorable and significant (see Matthew 21:12–13; Mark 11:15–17; Luke 19:45–46; John 2:14–17). It is worth recalling here in some detail.

Jesus went into the temple and saw the stalls of the money changers and traders in the Court of the Gentiles. Their trade was approved by the temple authorities but he found it deeply offensive. The money changers were making a profit by changing ordinary, everyday money into special temple coinage, which could be used for the offerings and to buy birds and animals from the traders' stalls for the temple sacrifices. To Jesus, their trading was symbolic of corrupt worship and a distraction from the prayer that the people of 'all the nations' should be free to offer in this house (Mark 11:17). In bitter indignation, he made a whip and drove both the traders and their animals out of the temple courts, overturning their tables and telling them, 'Take these things out of here! Stop making my Father's house a market-place!' (John 2:16).

Many, many years ago, in a school 'Scripture' lesson (as they used to be called), I remember our atheistic teacher telling us that in this event Jesus became so angry that he lost control of himself and more or less went berserk. Closer reflection, even as a not very religious teenager, led me to see the story rather differently. What Jesus expressed was not temper or frustration, and certainly not loss of control, but indignation and justifiable anger at what he saw as a corruption of God's purpose and a denial of God's honour. This was the temple, not a shopping mall; a place of prayer, not a place of trading. His actions, extreme as they were, were signs of his messianic authority. Malachi had foretold long ago that when the Lord 'suddenly came', he would 'purify' his temple (3:1–4). Now it had happened. This, surely, is the 'wrath of the Lamb' in action—not petty irritation or intemperate anger but the measured yet forceful expression of righteous indignation at the corruption of a holy place and the violation of sacred things.

I share a sense of horror at the violent images in these chapters of Revelation. Like most readers, I find them ugly and appalling. At the same time, I recognise that they stand for what we might dub an inconvenient truth—that the world is in desperate need of cleansing, and that it is inconsistent with the concept of a God of justice and righteousness for evil to be endlessly tolerated. The day must come when a good and just God calls a halt to evil, exploitation, cruelty, injustice and greed. Can we be surprised if that involves indignation and righteous anger? The Father of Jesus, like his Son, must be allowed to take a whip and drive out the evildoers who have corrupted and distorted his good creation.

On the evidence of these visions, the originating agents of corruption and evil are seldom human, but are malign forces—mental or spiritual—that afflict and torment their human victims. The angels who pour out the 'bowls full of the wrath of God' (15:7) are carrying out an operation of cosmic cleansing, at the end of long ages of divine patience during which mercy and forgiveness were on offer. Even at the very end, we shall see that mercy and forgiveness are still available for those who seek them.

In terms of the overall message of Revelation, with its

clear intention to reassure the Christians of the day that God has not forgotten them and that they can live in confidence and peace, these awful final visions might seem counterproductive. If I were looking for an answer to fear and anxiety, I wouldn't choose images of hideous frogs and scarlet monsters. However, the Christians of the early Church were not the children of centuries of Christendom. They lived under the shadow of Christ's cross; in Paul's phrase, they had 'died with Christ' (Romans 6:5–6), so what could a few green frogs do to them?

Not only that, but they saw, as we struggle to do, that conflict is not contrary to the gospel but right at its heart. Unless we embrace the idea of the 'crucified life' (Galatians 2:19–20), we shall never really understand the risen life. It is in the furnace of the day-to-day battle for holiness that Christians are tested and saints are made.

At the same time, as we shall see (and, indeed, as Revelation constantly reminds us, with its recurring visions of the throne room of heaven, where praise and worship surround the Lord of history) struggle and conflict end not in despair but in serenity and bliss. The conflict moves inevitably towards an outcome. That outcome is not heavenly bliss in the future; it's the joy and peace of fulfilment, promised now and (in the words of the apostle Peter) 'kept in heaven for you, who are being protected by the power of God through faith for a salvation ready to be revealed in the last time' (1 Peter 1:4–5).

The vision of the rider on the white horse in Revelation 19:11 in many ways sums up these arguments. This figure is the captain of the heavenly host in the final battle with evil. Heaven opens and 'behold, a white horse!' (RSV). He leads an angelic army, also clothed in white, the colour of purity. The rider has several titles: 'Faithful and True' are qualities, and they determine the way in which this final conflict will be waged ('in righteousness he... makes war'). He has a name inscribed which 'no one knows', but in fact we are told who he is: 'The Word of God' (v. 13). He is the Logos, the mysterious Word who was with the Father from the beginning, who shared in the work of creation, who 'was with God' and 'was God' (John 1:1), and yet who 'became flesh and lived among us' (v. 14). He is 'God the only Son, who is close to the Father's heart', the one who has made God known to us (v. 18).

In other words, the rider is Jesus, the Lamb of God, the crucified and risen Saviour, but now he has another task to fulfil. Having drunk the cup of human suffering and sin on the cross (remember 'remove this cup from me', Luke 22:42), he is now asserting the right and rule of God over the forces of evil that have held humanity captive for too long. So 'the kings of the earth with their armies' (Revelation 19:19) are judged and defeated. The beast from the pit is captured and thrown into the 'lake of fire' (v. 20). We now understand that the Lamb of God is also 'King of kings and Lord of lords' (v. 16).

That is surely the paradoxical meaning of this vision. The rider on the white horse is a conquering king who, in the name of God, will defeat and destroy all that is evil. His garments are spattered with blood—most probably his own, shed for his people, because the first mention of the blood comes before he engages in the battle.

The picture is, and is meant to be, terrible, overwhelming and utterly terrifying for those who have opposed God and defiled his creation. Yet for those to whom these visions were first related, and for those who read them now with faith, the picture is far from terrifying. The rider is the Saviour of the world, the Lamb of God who 'takes away' its sin, and that is exactly what he is about to do. He is taking away not simply individual sins or personal sinfulness but 'the sins of the whole world' (1 John 2:2)—cosmic evil. Christians are used to speaking of the 'finished work' of Christ on the cross, and of course that is true. All that was necessary for human salvation was achieved in that one epic sacrifice. But the application of his victory over sin and death, the working out of its consequences in individual lives and in history, has continued ever since, as people have responded to his grace and love and received its benefits. Now, as this vision reveals, that era is over. The long days of grace, in which salvation through Christ was freely offered and millions responded, is to end. The time has come for the final victory of the 'finished' work (see John 19:30).

The importance of all this for today's reader is its relevance to one of the most persistent accusations made by critics of the Christian faith—and one also often expressed, even if hesitantly, by practising Christians. How can it be that in a world created by a good and loving God, there is so much suffering and conflict, many of whose victims cannot on any just count be considered deserving of their fate? Every time there is a natural disaster—flood, plague, pandemic, earth-quake, tornado—the question is raised and honest Christians struggle to answer it. Every time conflict scars human flesh or destroys human lives, the same question arises.

In one sense, there is no answer, certainly not one that we can find for ourselves. Previous generations of believers, and perhaps some today, were more willing to see such events as divine judgment on human sin. John and Charles Wesley, for example, saw an earthquake in London in 1750 in those terms, and used it as an incentive to repentance. In every such case, however, it is impossible to argue that only the 'guilty' suffered. Thousands and thousands of the innocent suffer as well.

Revelation offers another way of seeing it all. Because God is just, there is judgment, but it is not indiscriminate or blind. Through all the pictures of suffering and conflict, the heavenly throne room is in control. More than that, the Lamb whose sacrifice has taken away the sin of the world shares in that judgment: it is the world's Saviour who is the world's Judge. The rainbow of the covenant of mercy fills the sky, the prayers of the saints ascend to the throne, and the rider on the white horse of judgment is Faithful and True.

None of us is completely innocent, of course. To a greater or lesser degree, we all share in the 'sins of the world' for which Jesus died. But these terrible pictures of judgment in Revelation are not directed at individual people; they are aimed at sin itself. The darkness that has hung over the whole of history is being challenged, judged and destroyed. The images are of injustice, greed, corrupt power, even outright rebellion against the Creator. Until they are identified, rooted out and removed, the creation itself is not what God had intended.

The process described in these visions and images, while

undoubtedly horrific and terrible, is absolutely necessary. Without it, God would be neither just nor mighty. Yet all the while, like a musical theme running through a symphony, we can hear the sweet notes of grace. Every scene of judgment is matched by a scene of mercy, peace and joy. The conflict and the suffering are neither pointless nor an expression of simple vengeance, but justice matched by love.

Many people who have been through times of great personal suffering have also experienced this paradox. Suffering seldom makes us worse people, and sometimes it creates saints. I recall the wife of a friend and colleague of mine who died in early middle age, leaving her with three children under ten. She had nursed him through three years of increasing weakness and pain until, eventually, the disease took its inevitable toll. She asked me to preach at his funeral and, a month or so later, wrote to me. In her letter she said that those three years had not been wasted. 'I wouldn't have missed the experience for the world,' she said. It had not been pointless—far from it.

Often, what worry us most in life are the moments when we feel we just don't know or understand what is happening. Humans have a great, inbuilt need to know. We can face almost anything so long as we have an explanation for it. The visions of Revelation can provide, for the eye of faith, images of explanation, ways of understanding. 'Don't be afraid' and 'Don't worry' are meaningless exhortations unless they come from someone who has grounds for confidence. The Lamb on the throne, the one bearing the marks of his suffering, is precisely that person.

The new Jerusalem

Revelation 20—21

These chapters draw the story of Revelation to a conclusion, with judgment of sin and joy for the followers of the Lamb. They describe both the cleansing of the creation and the birth of a new one; nightfall for the kingdoms of the world and a bright dawn for the kingdoms of our Lord and of his Christ.

Then I saw a new heaven and a new earth; for the first heaven and the first earth had passed away, and the sea was no more. And I saw the holy city, the new Jerusalem, coming down out of heaven from God, prepared as a bride adorned for her husband... I saw no temple in the city, for its temple is the Lord God the Almighty and the Lamb. And the city has no need of sun or moon to shine on it, for the glory of God is its light, and its lamp is the Lamb. The nations will walk by its light, and the kings of the earth will bring their glory into it. Its gates will never be shut by day--and there will be no night there. People will bring into it the glory and the honour of the nations. But nothing unclean will enter it, nor anyone who practises abomination or falsehood, but only those who are written in the Lamb's book of life.

REVELATION 21:1, 2, 22–27

Throughout the book of Revelation, John has been spectator and recorder of a kaleidoscopic series of visions. Hideous images of figures who personify opposition to God have passed across the cosmic stage—the dragon, various beasts, locusts, strange horses, green frogs. Then, as though to balance the scene, there have been wonderful visions of the white-robed saints and martyrs in heaven, angels offering worship, the sweet smell of the incense of the prayers of the faithful, and, seated on the great throne of the universe, God himself, with Jesus the Lamb beside him. All of this has inevitably moved towards a conclusion, which is recorded in these last two chapters of the book.

First comes the final judgment. Needless to say, the One on the throne has not been unmoved by the suffering of his people or the sin that is its root cause. He has waited while his angels call on people to repent—which many do (see, for instance, 11:13). Judgment is inevitable, however, for without it the God of the whole earth will be revealed as either powerless or compromised. Those who finally resist grace, who, right to the end, stand against his just and gentle rule, will not so much be judged by God as judge themselves.

There seem to be two judgments described in chapters 20—21. One is a judgment of people's deeds: they are judged 'according to their works, as recorded in the books' (20:12). The second is based on 'the Lamb's book of life' (21:27; see 20:15), which appears to contain the names of those who have confessed Christ, including many who have suffered in his name.

It's dangerous to try to build a systematic theology or doctrine on visions that require interpretation. Based on what we know of the teaching of the New Testament, however, the two judgments would appear to correspond to Paul's account of the way divine judgment works, in his letter to the church at Rome. There is, as he argues, 'no condemnation for those who are in Christ Jesus' (8:1)—those who, through grace, have received forgiveness and been justified. They must surely be those who are written in 'the Lamb's book of life', who bear his mark on their foreheads.

In an earlier passage in the same letter, however, Paul is concerned with those who have not had the blessing of 'the law' (that is, the law of God)—Gentiles, specifically. What of them? He argues that Gentiles in that position may 'do instinctively what the law requires' by obeying their consciences, and so perhaps be excused on the day of judgment (see 2:12–16). When the books of human deeds are opened (to use apocalyptic language), they will be judged 'according to their works'. In this way, divine justice is preserved for all, irrespective of nationality, culture or background. No one will be able to shake a fist at God and say, 'You weren't fair to me.'

Paul points out here that it is 'according to my gospel' that God will judge the world 'through Jesus Christ' (v. 16). The Lamb who redeems the world will also be the agent of judgment of sin. It is hard to imagine a more merciful approach to judgment than that.

Much the same picture of two judgments appears in the

teaching of Jesus. The parable of the 'talents' (Matthew 25:14–30) is clearly applied to Christ's 'servants'. What have they made of the precious gift of grace? The subsequent parable of the 'sheep and goats' is equally clearly applied to people in general ('the nations', in Greek *ethnoi*: v. 32). They are to be judged by their actions towards 'the members of my family' (v. 40).

The process of judgment, as described in Revelation, is rather confusing—but then, dreams and visions usually are. It speaks of two resurrections and two judgments, either side of a 'millennium'—a thousand-year span during which the saints 'reign with Christ' (20:4). Most biblical scholars now interpret this in a metaphorical rather than literal sense, as they do the subsequent battle with 'Gog and Magog' (v. 8), who are seen as personifications of opposition to the kingdom of God.

Time passes, its ages roll on, but in the end all comes to judgment. That is not, by any means, an ugly or horrifying end of things, for 'judgment' is another way of saying 'justice', or 'closure', a word popularly used to describe a proper completion of a painful event. Where God is concerned, 'justice' is another way of saying 'mercy'. Without the final judgment of evil, in which all its agents, in apocalyptic language, are thrown into a 'lake of fire' (20:14), there can be no kingdom of heaven, no holy city, no 'new heaven and… new earth' (21:1).

But there is! That is the glorious prospect introduced in the most memorable terms in chapter 21. The old 'heaven and earth' (the words simply mean 'sky and land') have passed away, to be replaced by new ones. Indeed, the voice of God from the throne declares, 'See, I am making all things new' (v. 5). This, at last, is the longed-for renewal of creation. All that is evil and corrupt has been removed. The spiritually 'thirsty', those who, however instinctively, long for the renewing life of God, will receive 'the water of life as a gift' (22:17). The One on the throne will be their God and they will be his children.

A quick tour of the holy city will reveal the ways in which it contrasts not only with the 'Babylon' of Revelation but with all the cities of earth. While the description is visionary and metaphorical rather than literal and physical, the over-whelming impression is of a place of beauty, splendour and delight—the sort of place we might accurately describe as 'heavenly'.

It is called the 'new Jerusalem' (21:2). The old one, central to the lands occupied by the Jewish people, was first conquered by the army of King David and a site was chosen for a temple to house the sacred ark that the Israelites had brought with them into Canaan long before. David's son, Solomon, eventually built a magnificent temple on this site, hoping that it would be a permanent centre for the true worship of Yahweh, the almighty God. Sadly, after his reign ended, the nation of Israel divided, with the ten northern tribes forming a separate kingdom and establishing other centres for the worship of the Lord, though Jerusalem remained a place of pilgrimage for all Jews.

During the centuries between Solomon and the days of the New Testament, Jerusalem was several times conquered by the Babylonians and Assyrians and the temple fell into disrepair. It was partially rebuilt in the time of Nehemiah, but on a much smaller scale. This temple was desecrated by the conquering Greeks in the centuries immediately before the coming of Jesus. It was not until the time of Herod the Great, at the end of the first century BC, that the magnificent temple of the time of Jesus was completed—only to be destroyed by the Romans in AD70, after a Jewish revolt against their rule. The disaster was completed when the Jews were expelled from their own land, and the temple remained a forlorn ruin at the time when John had his visions on Patmos.

This long history of city and temple, covering over a thousand years, explains the profound significance of the very name 'Jerusalem' to the Jews. Still today, at Passover, their prayer is 'Next year, in Jerusalem', and that fervent dedication to the concept of a holy city lies behind much of the political tension and strife in the region today.

So a 'new Jerusalem' was a splendid and thrilling prospect —a new centre for the worship of the one true God, a new tabernacle of his presence among his people, a focus for faith and adoration, a glorious vindication of the Lord's long purpose of blessing. However, this is no straight replacement for the geographical, earthly Jerusalem. She 'comes down from heaven', gloriously presented like a bride at her wedding (21:2). The Holy Place in the earthly temple represented, in a kind of sacramental way, the presence of God, but now God is truly and transparently present. The language is quite specific: 'See, the tabernacle [literally] of God is among mortals. He will tabernacle with them; they will be his peoples, and God himself will be with them' (v. 3).

Because God is now present among his people 'in person', as we might say, there is no temple in the city. At first, this may have caused dismay to John's audience: no temple surely means no place for the worship of God, no house of prayer, no centre for offerings and sacrifices. But a moment's thought will have made it clear: that is the 'old' way, and this is the 'new' Jerusalem. There is no temple because God is there, right in the midst of the city. The worship is centred on the heavenly throne—prayers and praise come directly to him—and beside him sits (in the language of vision) the Lamb, the single and unrepeatable sacrifice for sin of which Hebrews speaks (see 10:12). No more offerings and sacrifices will ever be required, because sin, guilt and punishment have been dealt with once and for all. God is among his people, not symbolically or sacramentally but in actual fact.

It also quickly becomes clear that the people with whom God will dwell in the new city are not just the Jews but also the 'nations', the *ethnoi*—the other 'ethnic groups', as we say (see, for instance, 21:24, 26; 22:2). This is a glorious and universal blessing, fulfilling the ancient promise that the temple would be (as Jesus reminded the crowds in Jerusalem) 'a house of prayer for all nations' (Isaiah 56:7; Mark 11:17).

This city, while open to all (its gates are 'never shut'), is surrounded by a massive wall. It is to be a place of supreme security—not against enemy attack, because the enemies of God have been destroyed, but in the sense that a home is secure, a place of human unity and concord. The gates of the wall are named after the twelve tribes of Israel, and its foundations bear the names of the 'twelve apostles of the Lamb' (21:14). In other words, the wall creates a home for the people of the old and the new covenants, Jews and Christians.

The vision offers a spectacle of absolute splendour—gates of pearl, streets of pure gold like glass, walls adorned with priceless jewels. We might be tempted to say, no expense spared. In fact, it is simply a picture of superabundance, a city greater than Solomon's or any other earthly empire, richer in everything that matters most.

As we have seen, the city has no temple because it doesn't need one. Equally, it has no sun or moon: God is its light and the Lamb is its lamp. It also has no night, the time of fear and anxiety, especially in the ancient world. Fear has been abolished. Perhaps for that reason, there is also no sea (21:1): the Jewish people had an irrational fear of the sea (think of all those references in the Psalms to the sea and its terrors, including sea monsters and so on). Above all, there will be no uncleanness. Nothing will be permitted entry that 'practises falsehood' (v. 27). Heaven would not be heaven if the ancient evils were given an entrance to it.

At the very centre of it all, symbolically, is the throne of God. It is his rule, his loving will, his presence that makes heaven what it is. He is its security and its promise of peace. The picture of God now is an essentially loving one. He 'will wipe every tear from their eyes'—banish every memory of earthly sorrow and disappointment—and 'mourning and crying and pain will be no more' (v. 4). In the new Jerusalem we shall be loved, and we shall love, as never before.

The heavenly Jerusalem, unlike the earthly one, has no problem with water supplies. There is a 'spring of the water of life' (v. 6), the 'living water' of which Jesus spoke (John 4:10). Literally, 'living water' is spring water, the sort that bubbles from the ground, compared to the kind of water you would find at the bottom of a well or in a water tank. It is water that not only enables survival but offers real refreshment and joy.

As well as this spring, there is a river of the 'water of life, bright as crystal, flowing from the throne of God and the Lamb' (22:1). It runs down the middle of the street of the city, on either side of which stands the 'tree of life', like the one that grew in the garden of Eden at the start of the whole story of humanity (Genesis 2:9). This tree has two unusual properties. In the first place, it produces fruit every month. We can imagine how that vision would have impressed a hardworking agrarian society of people who laboured each year for just two harvests. Secondly, its leaves are 'for the healing of the nations' (v. 2)—again, the *ethnoi*, the Gentiles, the people who have been for so long strangers to the promises of God. At last—and the thought is profoundly moving—the hurts and injustices and sufferings of the whole world will be healed by the leaves from the tree of life.

This is a reminder of how all-encompassing the vision of the new Jerusalem is. In a strange piece of celestial surveying, an angel measures for John the dimensions of the city. It covers over two million square miles—truly vast, incomparably larger than any city in human history. We could compare it to the 610 square miles covered by Greater London. The figure itself is visionary rather than mathematical, but it makes a telling point, not lost, surely, on its first readers. This city is big enough for all of God's people, past, present and future, Jew and Gentile. Heaven will never be full.

We might ask, what occupies the residents of the heavenly city? Are they to spend the whole of eternity doing nothing but playing harps and singing worship songs? It is that sort of thought that leads some people to wonder whether they really want to go there at all! Again, being wary of taking in a wooden and literal way the language of mystery and dream, it is worth noting that 'his servants will serve him' (v. 3, NIV): they 'do him service'. There will be activity—work, if you like—creativity and fulfilment in the heavenly city.

That is, more or less, the vision of the heavenly Jerusalem. It is not so much that we have gone to heaven as that heaven has come to us: the city 'comes down out of heaven'. God has come to dwell, to make his tabernacle, among his people, just as he did, in a different way, in the coming of Jesus, where exactly the same language is used: 'And the Word became flesh and tabernacled [literally] among us' (John 1:14). Now the long purpose of God has been fulfilled. He is among his people. He is their God, and they are his for ever.

Facing the darkness,
finding the light

Revelation 22

Right at the end of the book, Revelation reverts to the present. What did its visions, warnings and promises mean to those experiencing them before their final fulfilment? What response did they require from them, and what response do they require from us, as we, like them, await the coming of God's heavenly kingdom?

'See, I am coming soon; my reward is with me, to repay according to everyone's work. I am the Alpha and the Omega, the first and the last, the beginning and the end.' Blessed are those who wash their robes, so that they will have the right to the tree of life and may enter the city by the gates. Outside are the dogs and sorcerers and fornicators and murderers and idolaters, and everyone who loves and practises falsehood. 'It is I, Jesus, who sent my angel to you with this testimony for the churches. I am the root and the descendant of David, the bright morning star.' The Spirit and the bride say, 'Come.' And let everyone who

hears say, 'Come.' And let everyone who is thirsty come. Let anyone who wishes take the water of life as a gift... The one who testifies to these things says, 'Surely I am coming soon.' Amen. Come, Lord Jesus!

REVELATION 22:12–17, 20

We have come to the end of the book called Revelation, or the Apocalypse. What, we might ask ourselves, has it 'revealed'? We have come to it with our 21st-century questions and anxieties and with our cultural conditioning, as well as with whatever faith we hold about God, Jesus and the scriptures. What has been the impact of this exotic, elusive book on our understanding of God and his ways? It has set out to open the window on hard truths about human experience: war, violence, plague, famine, death. It has also exposed human sin: greed, power, exploitation and injustice. At the same time it has constantly offered us glimpses, and more than glimpses, of the joy and serenity of heaven, where the Lord God and the Lamb are enthroned and the saints and angels rejoice. Now, right at the end, in the vision of the new Jerusalem, the two scenarios are brought together, and in these last words of the book the reader is challenged about his or her response to what has been revealed.

Nothing is meaningless

I think there are six important principles about sin and suffering that emerge from these visions. The first, and perhaps most fundamental, is that nothing that happens to us or to the created world is meaningless. Although we live in a creation fraught by its own randomness—created by God through purposeful randomness, it seems—Revelation sees it as operating according to distinct values, which reflect the nature and character of the One on the throne. He is Yahweh, the God who appeared to Moses at the burning bush, revealing his nature as both personal and infinite— the eternal present tense, 'I AM'. Those distinct values that give meaning to creation include justice, righteousness and hope.

Justice lies at the heart of the divine order of things because without it we live in moral chaos. In fact, this value seems to be deeply rooted in our nature, reflecting the image of the Creator. From our earliest years we understand the meaning of such phrases as 'It's not fair', 'That's wrong', and 'That's right'. It's no surprise, then, to find that the same values operate on the cosmic scale. Our God is a God of justice.

'Righteousness' is a word that worries many people: they associate it with false piety and self-righteousness. In the Bible, however, it is a crucial word, denoting what God represents and requires. Righteousness is simply doing what God requires, and that, in turn, means living consistently with the Creator's purpose, going with the grain of his creation.

Hope is also a fundamental feature of the world as it is, because that is the way God has created it. As Paul writes:

The creation waits with eager longing for the revealing of the children of God; for the creation was subjected to futility, not of its own will but by the will of the one who subjected it, in hope that the creation itself will be set free from its bondage to decay and will obtain the freedom of the glory of the children of God. (Romans 8:19–21)

Whatever else Revelation may say to us, it always holds out the precious gift of hope.

Things are not out of control

Parallel to the notion that things are not meaningless is the second of the principles about sin and suffering to be found in Revelation: events are not out of control. We often feel the opposite about them, usually because we know that they are out of *our* control, and this is particularly true of natural disasters. When we feel overwhelmed by events (and every single one of us has felt this way from time to time), it may not seem very helpful to assert that God is still on the throne of the universe and in control. It doesn't feel like it.

That's what makes the several appearances of the rainbow in the apocalyptic visions so powerful. At various points the rainbow appears (see, for instance, Revelation 4:3; 10:1). The significance is that the rainbow, as we have already seen, is associated in the biblical story with the aftermath of the great flood. As the waters cleared and Noah and his family offered sacrifices of thanksgiving, God made a solemn promise to them and to all the human race in the future:

'When I bring clouds over the earth and the bow is seen in the clouds, I will remember my covenant that is between me and you and every living creature of all flesh; and the waters shall never

again become a flood to destroy all flesh. When the bow is in the clouds, I will see it and remember the everlasting covenant between God and every living creature of all flesh that is on the earth.' (Genesis 9:14–16)

Clearly this did not mean that there would never be any more floods on the earth, but it is a covenant promise that they will never again be used as instruments of divine retribution. That is a vital truth when we are trying to relate a world of physical risk to the purposes of a loving God. While God may use the consequences of such events, he does not arbitrarily orchestrate them, and certainly not as a means of punishment. We learn lessons (and, indeed, God may teach us some) from the incidence of totally undeserved and apparently random suffering—ours or that of others. But that is a long way away from saying that God causes them in order to teach us lessons.

Suffering is part of our humanity

The third important principle arising from the visions of this book is that suffering is part of being human. We may wish it were otherwise but we cannot escape the fact that it is so. In the words of Job's friend, 'Human beings are born to trouble just as sparks fly upward' (Job 5:7). The cross of Jesus is the divine endorsement of this understanding, and the constant image in Revelation of the Lamb bearing the marks of slaughter is the equally constant reminder of it. Right at the heart of the throne of God, as it were, is the image of human suffering. At the same time, however, it is suffering redeemed, and that is the ultimate purpose of God for all who bear the sign of Christ.

On the other hand, Revelation makes it uncomfortably clear that much of that suffering comes about not through natural and random events (like floods and earthquakes) but through endemic human sin. War is manifestly of human invention and much famine is, too, not to speak of suffering through slavery, exploitation and cruelty. In my experience, there is a real difference in attitude between people who suffer through natural disasters and those who suffer through human activity. The former often accept their situation stoically because they know that they are sharing a common human fate, suffering from events not only beyond their control but also beyond anybody else's. The latter often feel bitterness, anger and a deep longing for justice to be done and the guilty punished.

In a mysterious way, both of these aspects of suffering are caught up in the symbolic figure of the sacrificial Lamb of God. Jesus suffered an undeserved but real and painful death. The Son of God tasted the bitter cup of pain, rejection and injustice: 'the righteous for the unrighteous' (1 Peter 3:18). No one could have been more innocent than Jesus as he stood before his accusers. Even his judge, Pilate, found him not guilty of all the charges laid against him. There was no ground, he ruled, for the sentence of death (Luke 23:14, 22). Yet Jesus, described as 'innocent' by the centurion who stood before his cross (Luke 23:47), was crucified as a criminal. The Lamb upon the throne certainly knows all about suffering innocence.

He 'bore our sins in his body on the cross' (1 Peter 2:24), yet through this mystery he not only suffered so that our sins can be forgiven but he also judged them. The cross expresses the mercy and love of God, but it also expresses his judgment of sin. Jesus is, as we have repeatedly remembered as we have followed the visions of Revelation, the One who takes away the world's sin. But Revelation also reveals the Lamb's righteous anger at the evil that brings sorrow and suffering to so many people.

The Lamb also reminds us of another important aspect of human suffering. God is aware of it; he knows. When Moses stood before the burning bush in the desert of Sinai, he learnt a fundamental truth about the God of his fathers. Moses had fled Egypt because he was afraid of being held responsible for killing a taskmaster. In that action, he may well have been expressing frustration at the helpless suffering of his fellow Jews in the slave gangs building Pharaoh's treasure houses. They were the people of the God of Abraham, Isaac and Jacob. Where was that God when they needed him most? The people had cried to God. Had he not heard?

It was before the burning bush, in a defining moment in the religious history of the world, that Moses got the answer:

'I am the God of your father, the God of Abraham, the God of Isaac, and the God of Jacob.' And Moses hid his face, for he was afraid to look at God. Then the Lord said, 'I have observed the misery of my people who are in Egypt; I have heard their cry on account of their taskmasters. Indeed, I know their sufferings, and I have come down to deliver them from the Egyptians, and to bring them up out of that land to a good and broad land, a land flowing with milk and honey.' (Exodus 3:6–8)

We can notice the order: I have observed, I have heard, I know and I have come down.

In the arena of human suffering, there is nothing more palliative than the assurance that someone knows and understands how we feel. It is deeply reassuring in our darkest moments, when we feel that our cries and prayers and tears have been overlooked, to understand that God sees our situation, hears our cries and knows our circumstances.

Of course, it is the fourth element here that we generally find hardest to appreciate: 'I have come down.' We are accustomed to thinking of God as up above, transcendent, even somewhat remote from us. How, we wonder, can the Creator of the universe 'come down' to be present within it? Yet in the story of the Exodus we see that he came down to the Israelites in a very visible and practical way. He went with them across the Red Sea, set his pillar of cloud and fire to accompany their journey, and fed them in the desert.

In an even more personal and literal way, that is what God did in Jesus. In his Son he 'came down', shared our pain and circumstances, offered himself freely for our forgiveness, and was raised from death so that the sons and daughters of earth might share the risen life of the Son of God.

All of these ideas are implicit in the strange image of that 'Lamb standing as if it had been slaughtered' who shares the heavenly throne (Revelation 5:6). In him, human suffering is not abolished (for then we would no longer be human), but it is transformed. That is a profound truth, which most of us can begin fully to understand only when we have been into the unavoidable dark valley of the shadow, where we find the Shepherd-Saviour beside us.

The cleansing of the creation

While it is true that human suffering is not abolished in Jesus, that is the case only for the present. The whole story of Revelation moves to its glorious climax and, in that moment of God's victory, sin, suffering and even death itself are certainly abolished. This is the fourth principle emerging from these visions. The end of the story is the cleansing of the whole creation. As we have already seen, all that is abominable, unclean, false, violent and impure will be purged from the holy city (21:27; 22:15). How could it be otherwise? For our holy God to tolerate or compromise with evil and injustice would be unthinkable. In mercy he has waited, providing time and space for repentance. He has no desire for any to perish but for all to come to repentance (2 Peter 3:9), but in the end heaven will be heaven, and heaven, by definition, is a place without sin.

The purpose of God

The fifth principle that seems to shape the visions of Revelation is the purpose of God. Of course, in one sense, that principle runs through all the others, but it can also be seen as a distinct motivation for the whole book. Many Christians talk of God's 'plan', including, often, God's 'plan' for their own lives, but a much better word is 'purpose'. A plan sounds inflexible and prepackaged, but it is almost impossible to read the Bible and interpret it in terms of a divine plan for history. Did God plan the fall and the disobedience that destroyed innocence? Did

God plan the destruction of the temple and the dispersion of the Jews? Did God plan that his chosen people would reject his Messiah?

If, rather, we talk of divine 'purpose', it's easy to see how God's overall purpose could take each of those events and adapt in order to ensure that it was finally fulfilled. That is surely a more dynamic concept than the idea of a plan, which more or less requires the removal of any notion of choice or even individual responsibility. Revelation makes it plain that each of us does bear responsibility for our actions and their consequences. That was true for Judas Iscariot and the Emperor Nero, and it's also true for you and me, two millennia later.

The kingdom of heaven

That brings us to the sixth and final principle that runs through Revelation: the kingdom of heaven. It's a phrase very familiar to readers of the first three Gospels, where we could reasonably describe it as the message of Jesus in four words. It was what he proclaimed, it was what he portrayed in himself, and it was what he called his disciples to enter. For him, the kingdom of God (or 'of heaven' in Matthew) is not so much a place as a state of being—of living under the just and gentle rule of the Father. The kingdom of God was not, he explained, remote; nor could it be identified by outward appearances. 'The kingdom of God is among you,' he said (Luke 17:21). It is everywhere and anywhere that God's will is done. That is what Christians down the ages have prayed, in words Jesus himself taught them: 'Your kingdom come. Your will be done, on earth as it is in heaven' (Matthew 6:10).

In Revelation, the idea is shown in vivid pictures. There are other kings and other kingdoms, including Abaddon or Apollyon, who is king of the 'bottomless pit' (9:11). The beast has a kingdom, which he shares with other rulers, all destined to be destroyed in God's final judgment of evil (16:10; 17:12). One day we shall have the fulfilment of the words prophetically proclaimed by the seventh angel in John's visions: 'The kingdom of this world has become the kingdom of our Lord and of his Messiah' (11:15). It is the fulfilment of those words that is the true story of Revelation.

In contrast to the kings of the earth, whose power is arbitrary and temporary, in Revelation God is the epitome of true kingship: power used solely for good. His law is sweet to the taste, as the psalmist sings (119:103). His judgments are 'altogether righteous' (Psalm 19:9, NIV), and one day that just and righteous rule, exercised with faithfulness and mercy, will reign over the whole creation: 'King of kings and Lord of lords' (Revelation 19:16). The prophetic fulfilment of those words is unfolded in the final chapters of Revelation, although, as we shall see, the prophetic future has not yet become the grammatical present.

That is part of the mystery of time, which, like space, is the element in which we mortals live, although God himself, and therefore presumably the heavenly throne room of Revelation, is outside time. He is Yahweh; his holy name is simply the present tense: I AM. Indeed, his mysterious name could be translated 'the Existing One'. God has no beginning and no ending, because, unlike his creation, he is part of neither space nor time. God is not 'in' his creation: that is a ridiculous concept. It would be nearer the truth to say that the creation is 'in' God. Neither is he 'in' time, but 'inhabits eternity' (Isaiah 57:15). Both of those ideas are incomprehensible to human minds, I agree, but the logical alternative is a God who, like us, grows old and eventually dies, just as every star and planet, every tree and flower, and every animal and person will do one day.

The concept of a God who is both outside time and yet profoundly involved in it illuminates much of the Bible, and certainly the book of Revelation. It shows us visions that are both 'now' and 'not yet'. The truth of them is eternal and, therefore, true at this moment, as we read them, but in another sense the truth of them, though absolutely certain, has yet to be revealed. Thus the kingdom of God exists now wherever people accept his just and righteous rule, but it is 'not yet' in terms of its universal fulfilment. The prophetic future will become the ordinary, familiar, present tense.

Back to the present

In one way, the last paragraphs of Revelation 22, set out at the head of this chapter, take us back into that present moment. The new Jerusalem has not yet appeared; the return of Jesus to inaugurate his eternal kingdom still lies ahead. We know what the fulfilment of God's purpose will look like, but it hasn't happened yet.

So here we have a dialogue, as it were, between Jesus and

the Church, and between both Jesus and the Church ('the Bride') and the whole world. This conversation sets out the terms of God's generous offer to his human creatures. The new Jerusalem can be theirs; the appointed judge will also be their Saviour. All they have to do—though it will require the setting aside of prejudice, doubt and pride—is to come and drink (22:17). The water of life is gushing at their feet, cool and inviting. Anyone who wants to is welcome to plunge their cupped hands into the stream and drink from it.

This takes us back to those messages to the seven churches at the start of Revelation. The churches were deeply immersed in the troubles, trials and temptations of daily living, with the daunting task of remaining faithful in a world that was largely hostile to their beliefs. But throughout the messages there is this same note of welcome, this invitation to respond. They have not been abandoned by God—far from it. Even the lukewarm church at Laodicea is told that Jesus is standing at the door, knocking. All they have to do is open it and he will 'dine' with them, and they with him.

First, however, we must look more closely at these final words of Revelation. Quotation marks are a bit of a problem in the Bible, because they are not present in either the Hebrew or the Greek manuscripts, and this gives rise to mountains of scholarly debate. Where does the direct speech end? Who is actually speaking at any given moment? Here we have certain sayings in quotes, and most biblical scholars would assent to the translators' choices. Taking them as they stand, then, here are the verses from the end of Revelation set out as dramatic dialogue. If we read them in this way, we can feel the full force of their very positive and reassuring message to those who have just been exposed to the haunting, frightening and terrible visions of the apocalypse.

Jesus: See, I am coming soon; my reward is with me, to repay according to everyone's work. I am the Alpha and the Omega, the first and the last, the beginning and the end.

Narrator: Blessed are those who wash their robes, so that they will have the right to the tree of life and may enter the city by the gates. Outside are the dogs and sorcerers and fornicators and murderers and idolaters, and everyone who loves and practises falsehood.

Jesus: It is I, Jesus, who sent my angel to you with this testimony for the churches. I am the root and the descendant of David, the bright morning star.

Jesus and the Bride (the Church): Come.

Everyone who hears these words: Come.

Narrator: And let everyone who is thirsty come. Let anyone who wishes take the water of life as a gift.

Jesus: Surely I am coming soon.

Everyone who hears these words: Amen. Come, Lord Jesus!

The risen Jesus describes himself as 'Alpha and Omega', the very names applied to God himself in the opening paragraphs of the book: '"I am the Alpha and the Omega," says the Lord God, who is and who was and who is to come, the Almighty'

(1:8). Alpha and omega are the first and last letters of the Greek alphabet, and the clear meaning of these words, applied as a title, is that the one bearing it is both the beginning of everything and the fulfilment of everything—in other words (as it says) 'the Lord God the Almighty'. The unavoidable implication of such a title, as taken by Jesus, is divinity. The One who is Alpha and Omega is God—God the Father in chapter 1, and God the Son in chapter 22.

So the divine Jesus speaks to the Church, his 'Bride', but also to everyone who hears, and what he speaks is an invitation. The city of God stands holy and sanctified. There is no sin, no falsehood, no immorality or idolatry within its walls. Those already within it have been admitted because they have demonstrated their faith by their actions. As the earthly Jesus said, 'You will know them by their fruits' (Matthew 7:16)—how they live and the choices they make. They are not saved by what they profess, but by how they live that profession. They are already the disciples of Jesus, marked with the sign of the Lamb, residents of the city of God.

But the gates are not yet closed! The invitation still stands, and it is addressed, literally, to everybody: 'Let everyone who is thirsty come. Let everyone who wishes take the water of life as a gift' (22:17). No one who longs to be spiritually nourished, who longs for the life-giving gift of God, is to be excluded. Right to the end, the offer stands: 'Come'. Just as the Church pleads with Jesus to come back to earth to save us, so Jesus pleads with the people—the 'anybodies'—to come to the river of life and drink, so that they too may enter the holy city, the new Jerusalem.

It is not yet too late. It wasn't then, in the first century of the Christian era, and it still isn't now. The angel tells John not to 'seal up' the words of the prophecy of this book (v. 10). To 'seal up' is the final step before despatching a letter. 'Hold your hand,' he is told. Not until the appearing of Jesus in glory will the seals be applied. The time is near but, by implication, not yet. That time is still—is always—near, but it is still not yet.

There is a wonderful tension in these last paragraphs between the longing of the Church for Christ to come, for the final and total victory of what is holy over what is evil to be fulfilled, and an equal longing that, before he does come, more people will have turned to him for forgiveness and new life. When Christ appears, it will be, as the Apostles' Creed says, 'to judge the living and the dead'. The era of grace will not last for all eternity.

What we call the second coming of Christ has always been one of the core beliefs of the Church, enshrined in creed and liturgy, and marked every year by Advent in the church calendar. In recent decades, however, this aspect of Advent has been more and more neglected, certainly in the churches of Europe. This may be partly because the coming has been so long delayed that we assume it won't occur during our lifetimes. It may also be because the language of appearance in the clouds of glory and a day of judgment involving every person who has ever lived seems altogether too bizarre. Possibly, the traditional Advent emphasis on the so-called 'last things'—death, judgment and eternity—are not to the taste of a feel-good generation.

For those who harbour doubts or hesitations about the

second coming (and there will be few of us, I suspect, who haven't doubted, at some time or other) let Christmas be a warning. The coming of the Messiah had been long foretold by the prophets of Israel. Centuries had passed without any sign of this conquering successor to David whom they were expecting. He would be royal; he would restore the kingdom to Israel and usher in a reign of peace.

In due course, near the end of the reign of Herod the Great, after 300 years of enemy occupation, a tiny baby was born to a peasant couple. The place was right—Bethlehem—but everything else was wrong. He was not apparently royal. He was born not in a palace but in a stable. His parents were social nobodies. Throughout his life he consistently eschewed violence, said that his kingdom was 'not from this world' (John 18:36), and eventually submitted to death by crucifixion at the hands of the very Romans that the Messiah was supposed (in popular thought) to be overthrowing. When Jesus came the first time, in other words, it was not at all as people had expected, even though, when the prophecies are looked at with different eyes, he wonderfully fulfilled them.

If believing Jews in the first century could get it wrong, is it possible that believing Christians in the 21st might also be mistaken? Might it be that next time, whenever that is, he may take the world as much by surprise as he did the first time?

A contemporary poet, John Burnside, wrote a poem on this subject—a rarity for modern poets. He called it 'Parousia', which is the Greek word used in the New Testament for the second coming of Christ. In it, he first imagines the traditional dramatic appearing and then suggests a different way:

But I think, if it came, there would be something more subtle:
a blur at the corner of vision, a trick of the light,
or the notion that things have shifted
closer: streetlamps and walls,
privet hedges, trees, the neighbour's door
intimate…

Well, maybe, or maybe not. It is always futile to try to second-guess the ways of God. However, when Christians say, 'Christ has died; Christ is risen; Christ will come again', they are making an entirely meaningful assertion. The Messiah who died and rose will return to bring in the great conclusion of history. The seals on the letter will be fixed. The gates of the city will be closed. Time as we know it, and space as we inhabit it, will be transformed into something new and eternal.

The culmination of all this in Revelation is a striking vision of celebration—the wedding feast of the Lamb (19:7–9). He 'marries' his Bride, the Church—the vast, unnumbered community of those who have drunk the water of life, who have 'washed their robes', who have been marked with his sign on their foreheads. In marriage (the principle goes right back to Adam and Eve in Genesis 2:24), two become one. Christ 'becomes' his Church; his Church 'becomes' Christ. Now, the New Testament language about Christians being 'in Christ' and Christ being 'in' them becomes clear. They can never again be separated but will live in a wonderful unity of heart, mind and spirit.

The letter to the church at Ephesus uses the language of marriage to describe the relationship of the church to

Christ: '[He] loved the church and gave himself up for her, in order to make her holy by cleansing her with the washing of water by the word, so as to present the church to himself in splendour, without a spot or wrinkle or anything of the kind—yes, so that she may be holy and without blemish' (Ephesians 5:25–27). It is that same analogy which makes this passage in Revelation so vivid. Like a bride and groom at a wedding, or, perhaps more fundamentally, like a husband and wife in their continuing unity of relationship, Christ and his people, the Church, are united in faithful love.

Now, in these closing words of the book, the Lamb and his Bride address each other, and together address the world in its constant search for meaning and purpose. 'Come!' they say. 'It's not too late. The offer is still open.' Come, before the Lamb of God returns in glory.

*

Topics for discussion

Chapter 1: The human dilemma

1. Do you agree, in general terms, that we live in an extremely anxious age? Perhaps the group might care to draw up a list of common modern-day fears, putting them in some order of prevalence. Matthew 6:25–34 might provide a model.

2. Does the problem of undeserved suffering in a world that believers see as created by a good and loving God disturb members of the group? Is it something they have faced in conversation with neighbours or colleagues? The following chapters look in some detail at answers to this question, so it may be best to reserve detailed discussion of the topic until later.

3. Do you agree that our generation is more familiar than previous ones with cinematic and literary images of fantasy, allegory and horror, and might therefore find Revelation easier to read and understand than previous generations did?

Chapter 2: The defining vision: the risen Christ

1. Why do we think this vision of the risen Jesus is placed here in Revelation? Hebrews talks about people being

held 'all their lives… in slavery by the fear of death' (2:15). To what extent do we, or those we know, live our lives in conscious fear of death? Might it be true that while many people today don't often consciously think about it, it is the fear of death that drives them to seek any and every means of prolonging life?

2. What does it mean for us that Jesus has 'the keys to Death and Hades', with authority to release people from death and bring them to heaven? Does the vision of Jesus in glory clash in our thinking with the usual picture we have of Jesus on earth—the down-to-earth rabbi, the good shepherd, even the lonely figure on the cross? How would we reconcile the two?

Chapter 3: Key words in Revelation

1. This may be a difficult chapter to discuss, not because it doesn't raise questions but because it raises too many. 'Kingdom' and 'throne' may seem easy enough, but 'the Lamb', 'heaven' and 'angels' may pose more problems.

2. Most Christians are familiar with worshipping 'the Lamb of God, who takes away the sin of the world', but are we happy with the concept of a suffering—indeed, sacrificed—figure sharing the heavenly throne? What do people think about the idea of a God who has experienced suffering and has wounds?

3. Angels are common features in Christian art and hymnody. Has anyone in the group actually experienced the intervention of an angel in their life? The angels of God

do his bidding, but what do we make of the angels of Satan?

4. How do the group regard heaven? It has been suggested that Christians today seldom even think about it until someone close to them dies. If heaven as a place of ultimate bliss and fulfilment lies in the future after God's final victory over evil, as Revelation proposes, what exactly is our 'hope' here and now?

Chapter 4: Starting with the churches

1. To what extent (if at all) do the churches we belong to feel under pressure to compromise with contemporary moral or ethical standards? Can members of the group give actual examples?

2. Have any of our churches gone through times of discouragement? Symptoms often include an unwillingness to attempt anything new and an acceptance of gradual decline in numbers or of failure to attract younger members. What remedies do these visions offer?

3. Perhaps the most damaging of all problems is that of 'lost love'—for God and for each other. Again, have we seen this (in ourselves, or in a church)? What are its symptoms? What can rekindle a lost or fading love?

Chapter 5: Facing our fears: why do the innocent suffer?

1. What was your initial reaction on reading these chap-
    ters of Revelation: shock, horror, revulsion, awe? Taking
    the visions of suffering as a whole, can you see any way
    that they might serve to bring people to 'repent' (or do
    members find the very idea unacceptable)?
2. Is it true that disaster and suffering can induce a sense of
    awe? Have members of the group experienced this them-
    selves or in the lives of others? Is the 'innocence' of the
    sufferer an important factor, or is it irrelevant?
3. How do the group feel about the notion of a 'cause-and-
    effect' creation, in which God moves events and people
    according to a preordained plan? What part do we think
    human choice has to play in the purposes of God?
4. We have the promise here that God will 'wipe away the
    tears' of those who suffer (7:17). How would you respond
    to someone who suggested that it might be better if he
    just spared them the suffering?

Chapter 6: The cosmic conflict

1. In what way could our own experience of the Christian
    gospel be called 'bitter and sweet'? Cross and resurrection,
    repentance and faith, praise and penitence—how do
    these elements work together in our journey of faith?
2. In what ways might the idea of the 'inner holy place'
    provide hope and encouragement to Christians living
    in an increasingly secular society? When we talk of

opponents 'picking away' at the outer courts of the Church, where do we feel we have to draw the line?

3. Do you think of big cities as more ungodly than small towns and villages? What do you think are the positives and negatives about living in a city?

Chapter 7: Finding the safe place

1. Do you find the visions of the woman and her child, and of war in heaven, helpful or confusing? For that matter, do you find the whole idea of a cosmic conflict between light and darkness, good and evil, an important insight into the nature of our world? Does the spectacular battle between the angelic powers help or hinder your understanding of the lonely conflict of the cross and resurrection of Jesus ?

2. Perhaps more immediately, how do group members think these visions of conflict would have offered comfort and reassurance to the Christians of the early Church? In what ways can that comfort and reassurance also be ours today?

Chapter 8: The two beasts

1. In our rather different circumstances, how appropriate are the tests of endurance and faith when applied to issues of confrontation and compromise today? Faced with a largely sceptical and even scornful society (rather than a directly oppressive one), are our choices easier or

more complex than they were for the Christians of the first century? Can members of the group give examples of ways in which these issues of loyalty to Christ are tested today?

2. How do Christians today judge whether their response to a moral or ethical question is based on conscience rather than religious conditioning? How should they decide the issues that require them to take a stand? How helpful do you find the 'in his name' test?

3. If life is 'scarily unpredictable' (and it surely always has been) where is the calm centre for the believer?

Chapter 9: Babylon: money, power and might

1. Can we see signs of 'Babylon' (power used for selfish and sinful ends) in our contemporary society? Can Christians play a part in promoting a proper use of power and wealth?

2. If music, entertainment and colourful fashions are not in themselves sinful, how can we recognise when they are being misused? What tests might we apply?

3. How do Christians live in the world without being of the world (see John 17:14–15)?

Chapter 10: Conflict: the heart of the gospel

1. Do you agree with the idea that conflict is at the heart of human experience, personal and collective? Perhaps

some members of the group have examples to offer of ways in which conflicts, even painful ones, can lead to healing and new life when they are resolved.

2. How does the group feel about the 'wrath' of God? Did you find the picture of Jesus in the temple helpful in that respect? How do we distinguish between righteous anger and the destructive kind?

3. How can the 'finished work' of Christ for the salvation of the world offer hope to anxious and suffering people today? How do you feel about the idea that, in Jesus, God was dealing with the world's sinfulness as well as individual sins?

4. In the light of this chapter, how would you answer someone who asked you how a holy God could tolerate the presence of evil in his creation?

Chapter 11: The new Jerusalem

1. What do you think about heaven? Does this vision in Revelation help to answer any of your questions about it? As you explored the vision, combing through the pictures and images, did you find it attractive or rather daunting?

2. The last chapter was about conflict; this one is about closure—the judgment of evil and its final exclusion from God's creation. This is the end of the long journey of history. What aspects of it bring you feelings of relief and joy? Are there any that cause apprehension?

3. Is there one image of the new Jerusalem that particularly strikes you as significant, beautiful or moving?

Chapter 12: Facing the darkness, finding the light

1. Of the six principles, the one that probably invites most discussion is the claim that suffering is part of our humanity. Does this square with our experience of life and other people's? Do we agree with the suggestion that it is less difficult to come to terms with suffering from natural events, such as flood or earthquake, than with suffering caused by human sin?

2. How do you feel about the second coming? Long delayed, do you suspect that it's never going to happen? What difference does it make to life to believe that the Saviour will return (in some way) as Judge?

3. Finally, do you find it helpful to see the familiar Christian story in this wider context—having its culmination in the final victory over evil and the ushering in of the kingdom of heaven? Does this put some of our other concerns into perspective?

*

Bibliography

Marcus Maxwell, *Revelation* (The People's Bible Commentary, revised edition) (BRF, 2005)

G.B. Caird, *The Revelation of St John the Divine* (2nd edition) (A&C Black, 1984)

Tom Wright, *Surprised by Hope* (SPCK, 2007)

John Polkinghorne, *The God of Hope and the End of the World* (SPCK, 2002)

Pilgrim's Way

Journeying through the year with the Bible

Pilgrim's Way is for all those who would like to get to know the Bible better, but don't know where to start.

In this book David Winter has selected Bible readings for every day of the year, chosen from both Old and New Testaments, combining well-known and loved passages with less familiar treasures. Each day's reading is linked to helpful and straightforward comment, and concludes with a final thought to take away and ponder. Readings are themselves grouped into themes, linked to the seasons of the calendar and of the Christian year. An index of Bible passages provides a useful way of tracking down a favourite verse.

If we walk the way of Christian pilgrimage, either as a new traveller or a veteran on the path of faith, what can be better than having the guide book for the journey in our hands? *Pilgrim's Way* offers an excellent introduction to the Bible's wisdom, inspiration and guidance.

ISBN 978 1 84101 529 3   £9.99
Available from your local Christian bookshop or, in case of difficulty, direct from BRF using the order form opposite. You may also like to visit www.brfonline.org.uk.

ORDERFORM				
REF	TITLE		PRICE	QTY	TOTAL
529 3	Pilgrim's Way		£9.99		

POSTAGE AND PACKING CHARGES				
Order value	UK	Europe	Surface	Air Mail
£7.00 & under	£1.25	£3.00	£3.50	£5.50
£7.10–£30.00	£2.25	£5.50	£6.50	£10.00
Over £30.00	FREE	prices on request		

Postage and packing	
Donation	
TOTAL	

Name _____ Account Number _____

Address _____

Postcode _____

Telephone Number _____

Email _____

Payment by: ☐ Cheque ☐ Mastercard ☐ Visa ☐ Postal Order ☐ Maestro

Card no ☐☐☐☐ ☐☐☐☐ ☐☐☐☐ ☐☐☐☐ ☐☐☐

Valid from ☐☐☐☐ Expires ☐☐☐☐ Issue no. ☐☐☐

Security code* ☐☐☐ *Last 3 digits on the reverse of the card. Shaded boxes for Maestro use only
ESSENTIAL IN ORDER TO PROCESS YOUR ORDER

Signature _____ Date _____

All orders must be accompanied by the appropriate payment.

Please send your completed order form to:
BRF, 15 The Chambers, Vineyard, Abingdon OX14 3FE
Tel. 01865 319700 / Fax. 01865 319701 Email: enquiries@brf.org.uk

☐ Please send me further information about BRF publications.

Available from your local Christian bookshop. BRF is a Registered Charity

About
brf:

BRF is a registered charity and also a limited company, and has been in existence since 1922. Through all that we do—producing resources, providing training, working face-to-face with adults and children, and via the web—we work to resource individuals and church communities in their Christian discipleship through the Bible, prayer and worship.

Our Barnabas children's team works with primary schools and churches to help children under 11, and the adults who work with them, to explore Christianity creatively and to bring the Bible alive.

To find out more about BRF and its core activities and ministries, visit:

www.brf.org.uk
www.brfonline.org.uk
www.barnabasinschools.org.uk
www.barnabasinchurches.org.uk
www.messychurch.org.uk
www.foundations21.org.uk

If you have any questions about BRF and our work, please email us at

enquiries@brf.org.uk

enter